THE EPISTLE OF PAUL
TO THE EPHESIANS

An Exposition

THE EPISTLE
OF PAUL
TO
THE EPHESIANS

An Exposition

by
CHARLES R. ERDMAN

PREFACE BY EARL F. ZEIGLER

THE WESTMINSTER PRESS

PHILADELPHIA

5 6 7 8 9 10

Published by The Westminster Press®
Philadelphia, Pennsylvania
PRINTED IN THE UNITED STATES OF AMERICA

PREFACE

No writer of New Testament books has designed a more excellent "uniform" for the Christian than the one described in chapter six of The Letter of Paul to the Ephesians. And there are many other passages in this letter that have become household treasures, and guideposts for the members of the church.

The writer of Ephesians captures the reader's interest by declaring in no uncertain tone that he has had a revelation from God "which was not made known to the sons of men in other generations as it has now been revealed to his holy apostles and prophets by the Spirit." The reader soon discovers that this "revelation" concerns the church and its terrestrial and celestial mission down through the ages until the end of time. The church is the body of Christ. Into this body are to be brought, through faith in Christ, any and every member of the human race who are to "maintain the unity of the Spirit in the bond of peace." This body is to believe and practice "one Lord, one faith, one baptism, one God and Father of us all, who is above all and through all and in all." And this unity becomes possible as "grace was given to each of us according to the measure of Christ's gift."

The student of Ephesians soon recognizes that this is truly an "ecumenical" letter, and that it has a contemporary relevance that cannot be overlooked. To the people of the early church, Ephesians became their authority for admitting into church fellowship the hosts of "Gentiles" who had formerly been largely passed by on the other side. Will Ephesians become to us of our generation a challenge to revive our evangelistic zeal that we may not by omission or commission sin against the Holy Spirit who endows believers to be witnesses for Christ?

The man who wrote this exposition of Ephesians was Dr. Charles R. Erdman. By training and by practical experience he was endowed with the right kind of gifts to make Ephesians come alive for the reader and student. He was a seminary professor, a pastor, a writer of many books. Moreover, he had passion for furthering the gospel. There is a glow in his writing that reveals the Spirit pushing his pen.

Dr. Erdman was familiar with other scholars who have written commentaries on Ephesians. Some of these have questioned the authorship of Ephesians, and have concluded that it was written by some unidentified person other than Paul, possibly one of his disciples. Dr. Erdman, however, states his own view: "That the letter was written by Paul there should be no serious doubt." This conclusion as to authorship leaves Dr. Erdman free to interpret the many personal references to Paul in Ephesians in a way that would not otherwise be possible. With Dr. Erdman's help the present-day student of Ephesians can receive what was given to the early church readers, "So I ask you not to lose heart." And as these first- and second-century Christians studied, they knew that the church was ordained to last forever because its Head was the living Christ to whom had been given all authority in heaven and in earth.

In this age, Christians must be more than spectators. They must become actors in the divine drama that continues to unfold until every knee shall bow and every tongue confess that Jesus is Lord.

FOREWORD

The church of Christ, in its divine origin, in its present power for good, and in its eternal destiny, far surpasses the dignity and significance of any other society, organization, or movement known to man. One who holds a different view should read the arresting paragraphs of the following letter. He may come to realize that, with all its obvious imperfections, the church is proclaiming and establishing those principles of personal purity, of social justice, and of race relationship upon which the hopes of the world must rest. The primary message of the letter, however, is addressed to the members of the Christian brotherhood. It awakens in their hearts a hymn of praise for the unmerited mercies of God. It summons them to more devoted endeavor for the welfare of society, for the defense of the family, for the unity and growth of the church. It deepens their conviction that the gospel is designed for no one race or nation but as a message of life and of love for all the peoples of the earth. It inspires them with a more joyful confidence in the inexhaustible riches of redeeming grace revealed in Jesus Christ the Lord.

INTRODUCTION

Paul wrote the Epistle to the Ephesians while a prisoner at Rome. His long hours of confinement gave him opportunity for a wide correspondence with his Christian converts, and also for a grateful review of his own extraordinary career. He recalled the fact that as a bigoted young rabbi he had hated the Christian cause and persecuted the Christian church, but that after his miraculous conversion at Damascus he had been sent as a messenger of Christ to the Gentile world. He realized at once his personal unworthiness and the grandeur of his commission, as he wrote in this epistle, "Unto me, who am less than the least of all saints, was this grace given, to preach unto the Gentiles the unsearchable riches of Christ."

This mission he had proceeded to fulfill with heroic courage and unflagging zeal. He had preached in Damascus until compelled to flee for his life. Joining the Christian community in Jerusalem, he had been driven from the city by the mad hatred of the Jews. After a period of retirement in his boyhood home at Tarsus, he had been summoned to assist Barnabas in the work of the vigorous young Gentile church in Antioch. From that city as a starting point he had undertaken three notable missionary journeys. First he had visted the island of Cyprus and the central region of what is now known as Asia Minor.

On his second journey he had crossed to Europe and founded churches in Macedonia and Greece. As he turned eastward he had paid a brief visit to Ephesus, leaving there his new friends, Aquila and Priscilla. After a sojourn in Antioch he had returned to Ephesus and there spent three memorable years. Not only had he established in the city a strong Christian church, but from Ephesus as a center he had sent out messengers by whom

the whole province of Asia was evangelized and churches
were established in all its chief centers of population.
There at Ephesus he had formed the purpose of preach-
ing the gospel in Rome. He must first, however, visit
Jerusalem. Therefore after spending a few months in
Greece he had set out for Syria but stopped on his way at
Miletus, from which port he had sent for the elders of the
Ephesian church and bade them an affectionate farewell.

He had brought with him to Jerusalem an offering for
the needy Christians. The Jews, however, had been sus-
picious, and, mad with hate, had incited a riot in which
he nearly lost his life. He had been rescued by the Roman
guard and sent for safekeeping to Caesarea. There, held
as a prisoner, and receiving no justice from the Roman
rulers, he had exercised his right of citizenship and made
his appeal to Caesar. Thus at last he had reached Rome,
not however as an itinerant missionary, but as a prisoner
in bonds. His hope had been realized but under conditions of which he had not dreamed. All this and much
more Paul called to mind during the long days in which
he awaited his trial.

However, he had much else besides his memories to en-
gage him during his imprisonment at Rome. His confinement was not severe. He was allowed to dwell in his own
hired house and was permitted to converse freely with all
who wished to visit him. This opportunity as gladly accepted by great numbers of Christians who took counsel
with the beloved apostle and received from him encouragement for their own lives and service. It would seem,
too, that occasions were given to Paul for addressing other
groups composed of inquirers or of those who were curious
to hear the Christian gospel proclaimed by its famous ex-
ponent. It must have been in view of such opportunities
for testimony that Paul made, near the close of this epistle,
his earnest request for prayer: "Praying . . . on my behalf," he wrote, "that utterance may be given unto me in
opening my mouth, to make known with boldness the mys-

tery of the gospel, for which I am an ambassador in chains."

Thus Paul the prisoner was also Paul the preacher, the missionary, the courageous witness for Christ. However, during those years of imprisonment Paul accomplished much more than was possible by conference with friends or discussion with changing circles of visitors. He composed the immortal epistles which have come down to us across the centuries and comprise some of the most precious fragments of the past. They are of priceless value and contain messages of deep significance for the present day.

The reasons for the composition of these letters were various. For instance, a messenger had come to Rome bearing a welcome remembrance to Paul from loving friends in Macedonia. After a serious illness in the city this messenger, Epaphroditus, was returning home, and Paul sends with him a letter of thanks, in which he takes occasion to describe his experiences in prison and his confident joy in Christ. This composition is known as the "Epistle to the Philippians."

Then again word came from distant Colossae of serious heresies which were threatening the infant church, and to meet the danger Paul composed the famous "Epistle to the Colossians," which sets forth in such matchless terms the divine person and redeeming work of Christ.

By a strange providence a fugitive slave from Colossae had found Paul in Rome, had been led to Christ, and had become a beloved helper of the imprisoned apostle. This slave Paul wished to return to his master, Philemon. So he wrote the epistle which bears that name, and sent it and Onesimus the slave on the long journey eastward in company with Tychicus, by whom the letter was being dispatched to the Colossian church.

There were, however, other Christians dwelling in the same province with the Colossians whose interests lay heavily on the heart of Paul as he thought of them in his confinement at Rome. With these in view he composed the "Epistle to the Ephesians," taking advantage of the fact that this, too, could be sent in the keeping of his trusted messenger, Tychicus.

It is this historic connection with Philippians and Colossians and Philemon, and, more important still, its vital correspondence with the contents of these letters which confirm the belief that the epistle to the Ephesians was written by Paul about the year A.D. 63 during his imprisonment at Rome.

If as a result of his confinement nothing else had been accomplished by the apostle but the composition of this one sublime masterpiece, the church of all the ages would still have found, in this epistle alone, sufficient reasons for praising God, who thus ever can bring good out of evil and light out of darkness. The very production of this letter is a superb answer to the prayer of its author: "I ask that ye may not faint at my tribulations for you, which are your glory."

THE DESTINATION

This epistle was composed for Christian residents of the Roman province of Asia. This province stretched along the entire western coast of "Asia Minor." It contained many important and populous cities, of which Ephesus was the chief. From very ancient times this great metropolis held a place of prominence. It had been founded by Athenians but contained from the first a large percentage of Orientals. At the time of Paul it ranked with Alexandria and Antioch as one of the three great emporiums of the eastern Mediterranean trade. It was the commercial as well as the political capital of Asia. Its importance, however, was due in larger measure still to the religious interest which centered in the city. The temple there erected for the worship of the goddess Diana (Artemis) was one of the Seven Wonders of the World. This superb structure of shining marble stood facing toward the east, outside the city walls. It is reputed to have been four hundred and twenty-five feet in length and two hundred and thirty-nine in width and to have been supported by one hundred columns, fifty-five feet in height, each one a masterpiece of art and the gift of a prince. Its complete construction covered a period of two hundred and twenty years. Within its inner shrine stood an image of the goddess which was believed to have fallen from the sky. Behind this shrine was the treasury where kings and nations stored their wealth. It will be remembered that Paul's alleged interference with the craft of the silversmiths "who made silver shrines of Diana" and his supposed subversion of the worship of the goddess were the causes for the tumult raised against him which brought to a close his work in the city.

A second architectural feature of Ephesus mentioned in the Scripture narrative was the great theater, excavated on the western side of Mount Coressus, the largest in the Hellenic world, capable of seating twenty-four thousand five hundred spectators. To this theater the mob had attempted to drag Paul, and in it the riot was quelled by the wise counsel of the "townclerk," the recorder, the president of the senate.

It has been questioned whether Paul, writing from Rome, addressed his epistle to the strong church he had established in Ephesus, or whether he had in mind other churches and Christian communities as well. For the former view much can be said. It is the traditional view, reputed to have been accepted by the universal church, both ancient and modern. In the opening verse the phrase, "To the saints that are at Ephesus," is found in all existing Greek manuscripts but three, and in each of these it has been inserted at some time by some hand. The phrase is found in all the ancient versions of the New Testament. Furthermore, it was the usual custom of Paul definitely to designate his readers. It is improbable that no letter was written by the apostle to a church with which he was so long associated and which was of such importance in the accomplishment of his work.

On the other hand, it must be said that the words "at Ephesus" (ἐν Ἐφέσῳ) are not found in the two oldest and most valuable Greek manuscripts. These are older and of more weight as witnesses than the existing manuscripts of the ancient versions.

According to the testimony of the church fathers who wrote at a still earlier date, the manuscripts which they used contained no reference to Ephesus. In fact there seems to be no evidence that the phrase "at Ephesus" was found in any Greek text of the first three centuries. No local designation for the letter seems to have been found in any manuscript earlier in date than the latter half of the fourth century.

The still stronger argument against the theory that the letter was addressed specifically to the church at Ephesus is found in the character of the letter and in the peculiar relations which were sustained by Paul to the Ephesian church. These relations were particularly intimate and prolonged. Paul had founded the church and for some three years had been its devoted pastor. In referring to his interest for his Ephesian converts and his labors among them, he describes himself as ceasing "not to admonish every one night and day with tears." How strong were the ties of affection which bound him to this church is illustrated by that dramatic scene in which he bade farewell to the Ephesian elders. He called to memory their intimate fellowship. He warned them with loving solicitude. They were so overcome with emotion, so distressed at his departure, that they "fell on Paul's neck and kissed him, sorrowing most of all for the word which he had spoken, that they should behold his face no more."

It is hard to imagine that Paul could have written an epistle designed specially for these Christians without some reference to the long years he had spent among them, without some disclosure of his warm affection for them, without some personal greetings or some note of close acquaintance or grateful love. However, in this letter there are no local references, no personal touches, no indication of past intimacies. Indeed there are some passages which might seem to indicate that Paul had never seen these readers and that they had been ignorant of the exact character of his teaching and his mission. The profound and comprehensive statements and even the practical exhortations of the letter are abstract, philosophical, neutral, impersonal.

As a result of these arguments it has been concluded that this epistle was not addressed to any particular church but was an encyclical, or circular letter, intended for a number of churches, of which that at Ephesus was one.

Evidently most of the readers were Gentiles, and some commentators have gone so far as to suppose that the letter was a general encyclical to all Gentile converts throughout the Roman world. It is possible, however, to localize the destination with considerable definiteness. Paul sustains certain specific relations to his readers. He has heard recently of their faith and love; news has reached them of his imprisonment and they have been saddened by it, and are anxious to learn of its issue; they seem to be acquainted with Tychicus; they are distinguished by Paul from other Christians to whom they have shown love and for whom they are asked to pray. Furthermore, the letter is obviously a companion to the epistle to the Colossians, and is being dispatched by the hand of the same messenger, Tychicus.

It would seem, therefore, that it was intended for the Gentile converts in Laodicea, Hierapolis, and Colossae, and other cities of proconsular Asia, the province of which Ephesus was the capital. According to one form of this theory the words "at Ephesus" ($\dot{\epsilon}\nu$ 'E$\phi\dot{\epsilon}\sigma\omega$) were not found in the original manuscript. The sentence was complete without them. According to another form, the space they now occupy was left blank and was filled in with the names of the churches for which copies were made, or the blank was filled orally by Tychicus in each place where the epistle was read, and the name so supplied was then written in the copy left for that particular church.

This theory which regards the epistle as a circular letter makes it possible to identify it as "the epistle from Laodicea" to which Paul refers in his letter to the Colossians. Should this theory be accepted it is not difficult to understand how the words "at Ephesus" might have been inserted in the manuscripts, and why tradition has invariably called this the "Epistle to the Ephesians." Ephesus was the capital of the province. Its church was the most prominent in Asia. There the epistle would be read first. From there, probably, copies would be dispatched to the other churches. In this famous city the Christian community flourished long after most of the Asiatic churches had sunk into insignificance. It would appear that this theory best accounts for the various elements of the problem.

The question, however, is by no means vital, or even of very great importance. Whether this epistle was addressed to the Ephesians specifically and alone, whether it was designed also for the other churches of Asia, or whether it was an encyclical intended to be circulated through the province, the significant fact is this: that the letter contains a message of incomparable majesty and worth, adapted to the needs and the conditions of every Christian church in every age and in every clime.

THE CONTENTS

This is regarded as the greatest among the epistles of Paul; as "perhaps the profoundest book in existence"; as, indeed, "the divinest composition of man." Its majesty and sublimity have secured for it the title, "The Epistle of the Ascension." It concerns those "in the heavenly places." In its view it includes both eternities past and

those yet to come. The serenity and dignity of its spirit
and language are in complete harmony with the sustained
loftiness of its thought and teaching. It thus forms a striking contrast with the epistle to the Galatians. The reader
is conscious of entering a very different sphere. He has
left the realm of controversy for that of worship, the field
of battle for the house of prayer.

It is, however, as practical as it is sublime. Paul bases
the humblest duties on the noblest of doctrines. He insists
that truth must be expressed in life.

The substance of the epistle is a statement of the grace
of God to the church, and an exhortation to a life worthy
of Christians. Its emphasis upon divine foreordination
made this epistle a favorite with Calvin, as Galatians was
with Luther. Its treatment of the church as the body of
Christ allies this epistle to the Ephesians with its companion epistle to the Colossians. The latter fixes the thought
upon Christ the divine, glorified Head of his body, the
church; the former treats of the church, the body of Christ,
drawing its life from Christ, its glorified Head.

This church is viewed as a unique body in which God
had designed to unite Jews and Gentiles, and by which he
was to manifest before the universe the virtues and the
fullness of the divine life.

So prominent is this idea of unity that some have found
in it "the key to the epistle: the unity of the church of
God, the unity of the two great sections of the Christian
church, the unity of the members of the church catholic."

The supreme purpose of the epistle, however, is to establish the readers in their Christian faith; to guard them
against the peril of slipping back into their former practices
and, also, against the danger of forgetting as Jews and
Gentiles their unity in the body of Christ.

The epistle is divided into two great sections of three
chapters each. The first is doctrinal; the second is practical or hortatory. The first deals with Christian truth; the
second with Christian life. The first sets forth the grace

of God; the second is composed of exhortations to the recipients of this grace.

As was customary with Paul, the epistle opens with a salutation, a thanksgiving, and a prayer. Here following the salutation (ch. 1:1-2) the thanksgiving develops into a doctrinal statement of the spiritual blessings foreordained by God the Father, communicated through God the Son, and sealed to believers by God the Spirit, and all to the praise of the glory of his grace. It is "a creed soaring into an impassioned psalm." (Vs. 3-14.)

Then adoration passes into petition, as Paul prays that his readers may be given a fuller knowledge of their privileges, and particularly of the power of God graciously granted them. Then again petition passes into instruction as this power of God is illustrated by the resurrection of Christ, by his ascension, and by his being made supreme in the universe and Head of the church. (Vs. 15-23.)

The second chapter develops this doctrinal statement by showing how this same power of God, granted in grace to believers, secures for them a similar threefold experience: of resurrection from spiritual death; of ascension to a spiritual sphere, "in the heavenly places"; and of power to do good works and to manifest the grace of God in ages to come. (Ch. 2:1-10.)

This life has been granted not only to Jews, but, what is more remarkable, to Gentiles. The latter had not shared in the covenants, the hope, the life of God. But now privilege and separation are ended. Christ by his death has broken down the barrier, erected by the law, that divided Jews and Gentiles. He has brought both together in one body. Through him both have access as sons to the Father. They form one commonwealth, one family. They are being built together as one temple, founded on the apostles and prophets, with Christ Jesus as the great Cornerstone. In vital contact with him, Gentiles as well as Jews are incorporated in this holy sanctuary which is being erected for the spiritual indwelling of God. (Vs. 11-22.)

Paul is about to pray for his readers, but the mention of himself as the messenger to the Gentiles makes him pause to dwell upon the fact that the Gentiles are, equally with the Jews, heirs of the inheritance, members of the body, and partakers of the promise. This truth has been hidden from former generations, but now has been revealed to the apostles and prophets. The special privilege of proclaiming this truth has been committed to Paul. Unworthy as he believes himself to be, he has been given the authority to preach to the Gentiles the unsearchable riches of Christ, and to make all men know this great truth that God has chosen a universal church to make known even to the angelic powers his divine wisdom. This wisdom is manifest in Christ, and believers are examples of it in their freedom of access to the Father. The readers therefore should not be fainthearted because of the imprisonment and sufferings of the apostle, which are incidents involved in his proclaiming the reception of the Gentiles into the body of Christ. (Ch. 3:1-13.)

The prayer which was to have been uttered when the chapter opened is now expressed. It is addressed to the universal Father. It requests that the readers may be given spiritual strength, so that Christ may dwell in their hearts, so that they may realize the greatness of the love of Christ which ever transcends knowledge, so that through them may be exhibited the fullness of the divine life. (Vs. 14-19.)

The first great section of the epistle closes with a doxology. All the instructions which Paul has sought to impart in these three chapters have been voiced in thanksgiving and prayer. Naturally the petitions now swell into a majestic ascription of praise, celebrating the power of God, a power already manifested in believers but a power surpassing all prayer and thought. To him may glory be paid by Christ and his church, forever and ever. Amen. (Vs. 20-21.)

The practical or hortatory section of the epistle is comprised in the last three chapters. These exhortations deal, first of all, with the life of members of the church. They should live worthy of their position in a society the essential character of which is unity. This unity, however, is consistent with a large variety of gifts granted to his church by the ascended Christ. These gifts are designed to produce unity of faith and maturity of knowledge, and steadfastness in belief, so that the whole body, deriving its nourishment from the Head, may grow to maturity and be perfected in love. (Ch. 4:1-16.)

The next series of exhortations deals with the moral conduct of Christians as members of society. (Chs. 4:17 to 5:21.) As when dealing with life in the church the cardinal virtue was unity, so here the virtues emphasized relate to purity and holiness.

1. Believers are not to walk as did the Gentiles in delusion, ignorance, and impurity, but rather according to the principles of Christ. They are to put away the old life, the old self, "the old man," and to "put on the new man." (Ch. 4:17-24.)

2. In contrast with the vices of the old life, Christians are to manifest truthfulness, forgiveness, patience, good deeds, and purity of speech, and are to walk in love. (Chs. 4:25 to 5:2.)

3. Avoiding the impurity and covetousness which were outstanding characteristics of Gentiles, believers are to "walk as children of light." (Ch. 5:3-14.)

4. Instead of living in folly and excess, they are to walk in wisdom and to be filled with the Spirit of God, giving expression to their thankfulness in hymns of holy joy. (Vs. 15-21.)

The third series of admonitions relates to life in the family. The Christian household is treated as a type of the church. At least its members are all to live worthily of their membership in the body of Christ. Their spiritual equality is not inconsistent with submission and subjection and obedience. Wives are to be in subjection to their husbands; children are to obey their parents; servants are to be obedient to their masters. However, it is to be in every case a relation of mutual love. As in dealing with life in the church, Paul emphasizes unity, and as the supreme characteristic of life in the community is purity, so in the Christian family all relationships are made perfect by the continual reign of love. (Chs. 5:22 to 6:9.)

The last exhortations, which practically summarize the whole teaching of the epistle, represent the Christian life as a spiritual warfare. The conflict is not with mere human foes, but with unseen forces of evil. To fight victoriously one must avail himself of strength secured by union with Christ, and he must put on all the various pieces of armor which God provides. There is the girdle of truth, "the breastplate of righteousness," sandals to give a firm foothold furnished by "the gospel of peace," "the shield of faith," "the helmet of salvation," and "the sword of the Spirit, which is the word of God." Prayer there must be, and watchfulness and patient perseverance. Petitions must be offered continually for fellow Christians, and particularly for the apostle, that he may deliver with increased freedom of utterance the truth revealed in the gospel for which he is "an ambassador in chains." (Ch. 6:10-20.)

The epistle closes with an assurance that Tychicus, who bears the letter, will bring full information as to the situation and condition of the apostle, with a prayer for peace and love and faith, and with a final benediction of grace to all that love Christ. (Vs. 21-24.)

THE OUTLINE

I

THE SALUTATION

Eph. 1:1-2

1 Paul, an apostle of Christ Jesus through the will of God, to the saints that are at Ephesus, and the faithful in Christ Jesus: 2 Grace to you and peace from God our Father and the Lord Jesus Christ.

The epistles of Paul usually open with a salutation, a thanksgiving, and a prayer. In some instances the salutation or the prayer is omitted. Sometimes they are combined. In this epistle all three are present, and each one is complete, significant, and rich in meaning. Each is contained in a single sentence, yet these sentences are so long and so comprehensive that they fill an entire chapter and form an admirable introduction to the epistle.

The salutation follows the usual method of letter writing in the days of the apostle, and contains designations of the author and of the readers and also a personal greeting.

Here the author is described as "Paul, an apostle of Christ Jesus through the will of God." That the letter was written by Paul there should be no serious doubt. Its great conceptions, its tone, the manner of its teachings are all characteristic and unique, and all would point definitely to the great "apostle of Gentiles" even though he had not been named. It is true that it differs in temper from epistles like the Galatians. It is free from passion and controversy; it is more tranquil in spirit, more sublime in its thought. Yet such differences are to be attributed to changes of time and circumstances and to the specific aims of the writer.

Paul was in prison. His matchless sufferings and cease-

less toil had made him old before his time. What he had
endured for Christ was intimated in a letter written some
years earlier. "Of the Jews five times received I forty
stripes save one. Thrice was I beaten with rods, once was
I stoned, thrice I suffered shipwreck, a night and a day
have I been in the deep; in journeyings often, in perils of
rivers, in perils of robbers, in perils from my countrymen,
in perils from the Gentiles, in perils in the city, in perils in
the wilderness, in perils in the sea, in perils among false
brethren; in labor and travail, in watchings often, in hunger and thirst, in fastings often, in cold and nakedness.
Besides those things that are without, there is that which
presseth upon me daily, anxiety for all the churches."

Now he was confined at Rome. He called himself "Paul
the aged." He was not certain whether his confinement
would issue in release or in death. He was viewing all the
experiences of time in the light of eternity. He was writing of the dignity and glorious destiny of the church of
Christ. Comparison of this with his other epistles makes
certain that it came from the same mind and heart, and its
contrasts make it equally evident that it stands supreme
among all the writings of Paul. He now had been disci-
plined in the school of suffering and of service; and it is by
such training that spiritual maturity is usually attained.

Paul styles himself "an apostle of Christ Jesus." An
apostle is a messenger, "one who is sent." Paul regarded
himself not only as belonging to Christ but as having been
commissioned by Christ. He fulfilled the conditions of
apostleship, not only because inspired as a teacher and empowered to work miracles, but because he had seen the
risen Christ and by him had been appointed to his task.
This task was specifically that of testifying for Christ to the
Gentile world. This sense of the Lordship of Christ and
this belief that he was an apostle of Christ explain Paul's
notable life. Such submission to the divine Master and
such a belief that each task is assigned by him give dignity
to every character and nobleness to every career.

Paul adds that his apostleship was "through the will of God." In some of his letters he omits the phrase in this connection. In others he adds to it great emphasis. Here the words may be understood to convey either or both of two great conceptions. The first is that of authority; the second is that of humility. The first would lay further stress upon the thought of divine vocation. If Paul is an apostle "through the will of God," then his readers will do well to give heed to his words as spoken by one whose mission is divine.

The second conception is that the words convey an expression of humility. Paul realizes that he is unworthy to be an apostle of Christ. His high privilege has been granted through the grace of God. As he insists later on in the epistle, "Unto me, who am less than the least of all saints, was this grace given, to preach unto the Gentiles the unsearchable riches of Christ."

Both these conceptions should be familiar to the followers of Christ. If they are divinely called to their work, if their appointment is "through the will of God," then they should be fearless in the presence or before the opposition of men. On the other hand, if they realize their actual imperfection and weakness, the servants and messengers of Christ will be free from self-confidence and pride.

The letter is addressed "to the saints that are at Ephesus, and the faithful in Christ Jesus." "Saints" is the term usually employed by Paul to designate Christians. It did not signify any particular group of believers, but all members of the church in general. The primary meaning of the word is "separation." It is the same as the word "holy." Anything "set apart" for a special purpose could be called "holy." There was, however, one particular kind of separation with which "holiness" became associated, namely, "separation unto God." "Saints," therefore, described persons who were so set apart. They were "God's people."

Originally the word did not imply moral qualities.

However, when applied to the people of God it became associated with those virtues which are becoming to saints, such as purity and devotion and godliness, so that the notion of personal holiness became attached to the term. Not every saint possessed all the Christian virtues, nor did any one manifest them in perfection. It was "the language of charitable presumption." No individual completely answered the description, yet all were supposed to be striving toward the ideal expressed.

Therefore when the New Testament speaks of "saints," the reference is, not to persons who have attained rare heights of sanctity, or to those who practice certain conventional moralities or belong to distinct religious communities, but rather to the whole church of Christ, or to any one group of Christians. However, the very term implies that those to whom the name is applied should live as becomes the "people of God."

These saints were "at Ephesus." At least, some of them were. It is believed that the words translated "at Ephesus" were not found in the original text. Some very ancient authorities omit them. Then, too, the character of the epistle is regarded as too impersonal and too lacking in local color to have been addressed to a body of believers so near to the heart of Paul as was the Ephesian church. It is easier to imagine reasons why the words may have been added than to understand why they should have been omitted if written by Paul. If they were not in the original text, then it is supposed that the epistle was a circular letter addressed to certain churches in the Roman province of Asia, and as Ephesus was the capital the name of this city became attached to the letter and was introduced into the text of the salutation.

It is true, however, that the words "at Ephesus" are found in all but three existing Greek manuscripts, in the writings of the church fathers, and in all the ancient versions of the New Testament.

In any event, there were saints at Ephesus. This is the

important point. The interest should not center on the reading of a Greek text, but on a historic fact. Paul did establish a church at Ephesus. And what was Ephesus? It was for Asia the very center and focus of idolatry, of superstition, of wealth, of luxury, and of vice. In such surroundings a church was founded, and upon this church the fame of Ephesus will depend when men have forgotten all the wonders of that city and of the world. It is well to be reminded that spiritual states are not dependent upon physical conditions. Servants of Christ may be found dwelling near to the shrine of Diana.

The readers of the epistle are further defined as "the faithful in Christ Jesus." The "faithful" are not merely those who believe in Christ, but those who are faithful because of their belief, and are true to their faith. It denotes those who are steadfast in their Christian life and profession. Furthermore, the phrase, "in Christ Jesus," is to be understood as usually employed by Paul. It denotes a vital union and fellowship with Christ. Possibly it is the most significant and characteristic of all the phrases used by the apostle. He conceives the whole Christian life as being lived "in Christ." So here the spiritual constancy and fidelity of these readers is regarded as due to their relationship to their Lord. They not only believe in him and are faithful to him, but they are in him. He is the very sphere of their existence; he forms the sum and substance of their being. For them "to live is Christ."

For these readers Paul breathes his prayer, "Grace to you and peace from God our Father and the Lord Jesus Christ." This Christian greeting follows the two forms of salutation used by the Greeks and by the Hebrews in their letters, yet it combines and glorifies them both. The Greek "rejoice" is replaced by the Christian term "grace," which signifies the free, unmerited favor of God; this will impart all needed spiritual blessings. It will result in "peace," the Hebrew greeting which implied tranquillity and satisfaction of soul. Thus phrases of conventional courtesy are transformed by the apostle into a comprehensive Christian blessing.

This grace and peace have their origin and are expected to come from "God our Father and the Lord Jesus Christ." The union of these titles indicates that Paul regarded Christ as equal with God or as sustaining a unique relationship to him. The distinction between them which is here intimated is not in their nature, nor in their ability to bless. Grace and peace find in them a common source. The distinction is in the relation sustained to them by believers. God is their "Father"; Christ their "Lord." The word "Father" is used here with its distinctively Christian meaning. While it is true that in one sense God is the Father of all men, and the New Testament does recognize this universal Fatherhood, yet usually, as here, the word "Father" denotes the relation which God sustains to those who are his sons by "adoption," his children by a "new birth."

To these same persons Christ is "Lord." He is the Head of the church in which they are members. He has a right to their submission and trust. All who admit the supreme Lordship of Christ can enjoy in its fullest sense the Fatherhood of God. By all such believers grace and peace may be claimed. To all such believers this letter, in a real sense, is addressed.

II
TEACHING CONCERNING
THE GRACE OF GOD
Chs. 1:3 to 3:21

A. THE THANKSGIVING   Ch. 1:3-14

3 Blessed be the God and Father of our Lord Jesus Christ, who hath blessed us with every spiritual blessing in the heavenly places in Christ: 4 even as he chose us in him before the foundation of the world, that we should be holy and without blemish before him in love: 5 having fore-ordained us unto adoption as sons through Jesus Christ unto himself, according to the good pleasure of his will, 6 to the praise of the glory of his grace, which he freely bestowed on us in the Beloved: 7 in whom we have our redemption through his blood, the forgiveness of our tres-passes, according to the riches of his grace, 8 which he made to abound toward us in all wisdom and prudence, 9 making known unto us the mystery of his will, according to his good pleasure which he purposed in him 10 unto a dispensation of the fulness of the times, to sum up all things in Christ, the things in the heavens, and the things upon the earth; in him, I say, 11 in whom also we were made a heritage, having been foreordained according to the purpose of him who worketh all things after the counsel of his will; 12 to the end that we should be unto the praise of his glory, we who had before hoped in Christ: 13 in whom ye also, having heard the word of the truth, the gos-pel of your salvation,—in whom, having also believed, ye were sealed with the Holy Spirit of promise, 14 which is an earnest of our inheritance, unto the redemption of God's own possession, unto the praise of his glory.

Paul usually begins his epistles with a thanksgiving. Here, when the theme has been sounded, it is developed into a hymn of praise unsurpassed in majesty and splendor. The theme is the redeeming grace of God manifest toward the church of Christ. The hymn consists of three stanzas or strophes. The first relates to the past; the second to the present; the third to the future. The subject of the first is God the Father; of the second, God the Son; of the third, God the Holy Spirit. The division of the stanzas is marked by the refrain with which each one is closed: "To the praise of the glory of his grace"; "Unto the praise of his glory"; "Unto the praise of his glory." The three stanzas are bound into a harmonious unity by the recurring references to Christ: "In him"; "In whom"; "In the Beloved"; "Through Jesus Christ"; "In Christ." If the thirteenth chapter of First Corinthians is rightly celebrated as Paul's "Hymn of Love," this opening thanksgiving in the Epistle to the Ephesians may properly be designated as Paul's "Hymn of Grace."

The theme is expressed and the whole psalm is summarized in the initial verse: "Blessed be the God and Father of our Lord Jesus Christ, who hath blessed us with every spiritual blessing in the heavenly places in Christ" (v. 3).

God is declared "blessed" because he "hath blessed us." Evidently here the word "blessed" is used in a double sense. As is commonly said, men can bless God only by words and thoughts; he blesses men by acts of love and grace. Yet is it not true also that, in addition to our words and thoughts and hymns of praise, we can express our gratitude by deeds of mercy and kindness done to others in a spirit of thankfulness to God?

Here God is described as "the God and Father of our Lord Jesus Christ." The thought of God as the Father of Christ is quite familiar. It should be remembered, however, that Christ was a Son in such a unique sense that he "called God his own Father, making himself equal with God." On the other hand, as true man, Christ recognized God as his God quite as really as his Father. He habitually prayed to God. On the cross he cried in agony, "My

God, my God, why hast thou forsaken me?" In resurrection triumph he declared, "I ascend unto . . . my God." The mystery of such a union cannot be explained; but Christ was at once human and divine.

The blessings for which Paul expresses praise are defined as to their nature, the sphere in which they are enjoyed, and the condition on which they are received.

As to their nature, they are "spiritual." Men properly "praise God from whom all blessings flow"; but the blessings Paul here has in mind are not physical, material, temporal. They are the gifts of grace which the following verses describe. They include adoption as sons of God, forgiveness of trespasses, the sealing of the Holy Spirit, the assurance of eternal glory.

These blessings are experienced "in the heavenly places," to which believers are now raised by faith in Christ. The phrase is peculiar. It appears five times in this epistle and nowhere else in the New Testament. It describes the sphere to which Christians belong, the heavenly realm in which they are already seated, the place which they are to hold against all the assaults of the evil one. These heavenly places are not remote or future; nor are they merely the region from which blessings come. They are rather the heaven which even now lies within and about the followers of Christ.

Therefore the phrase "in Christ" is added. It is the most important phrase of the epistle. Its full force is felt here. All these blessings have been designed for those who are in fellowship with Christ, who belong to him, who are one with him. To be blessed "with every spiritual blessing in the heavenly places" one must be "in Christ." (V. 3.)

Such is the theme of the hymn, namely, the blessings which come to those who belong to Christ. The first stanza now turns to the past. It traces these blessings to an eternal purpose. It states that they are in accordance with the divine choice. This choice was exercised "in

Christ." It was in view of his relation to believers and his work for believers. "He chose us in him before the foundation of the world."

This election was, therefore, before all time. It was an act of the divine mind. It was not determined by any foreseen virtue or goodness in its objects. Such qualities were rather the purpose which God had in view, namely, "that we should be holy and without blemish before him in love." God intended that those who were chosen "in Christ" should be "holy ones," "saints," "consecrated" to him. He designed that they should be free from moral fault. He purposed that they should live in a spirit of "love." Those who truly belong to Christ will endeavor to fulfill this divine intention and to realize this divine ideal which in the future is to be perfectly attained.

The reason for the election of believers is traced to a predestinating act of God, "having foreordained us unto adoption as sons." Thus as the election was intended to secure for believers holiness of character, so the foreordination was with a view to granting them a blessed standing or position. The word translated "adoption as sons" is peculiar to Paul. It expresses a particular relation to God, implying special privileges of access and communion and also the rights of inheritance. It is an idea borrowed from Roman law. According to this provision one who was a stranger in blood became a member of the family into which he was adopted, and had all the rights and privileges which would have been his had he been a son by birth.

"Sonship" therefore describes the standing or the status of a Christian. It is the rank to which God admits those who believe in his Son. Furthermore, it has been made possible only by the work of his Son. It is "through Jesus Christ." Only when redemption had been accomplished was sonship possible. "God sent forth his Son . . . that he might redeem them that were under the law, that we might receive the adoption of sons. And because ye are sons, God sent forth the Spirit of his Son into our hearts, crying, Abba, Father." (Gal. 4:4-6.)

The privileges which adoption now confers, the access to God and the conscious acceptance with him, are to have a glorious consummation at the coming of Christ when the bodies of believers are to be made glorious and immortal, to correspond with the perfected state of the heirs of God who are to be partakers of his eternal glory. In this sense we Christians are yet "waiting for our adoption, to wit, the redemption of our body" (Rom. 8:23).

This adoption is said to be "unto himself," that is, unto God. Thus God's intention in foreordaining us to the status of sons is to bring us to himself, into true and perfect and adoring fellowship with him who is the source and giver of all life and blessedness and joy.

This adoption is stated further as being "according to the good pleasure of his will." This denotes the kind intent, the gracious purpose of God. It emphasizes the fact that the election and foreordination of God are not due to human merit, but have their source wholly in the sovereign will and goodness and love of God.

Finally and supremely, this election and foreordination are declared to be "to the praise of the glory of his grace." This was their ultimate purpose and design, namely, that thereby the splendor and magnificence of the grace of God might be manifested and adored. "Glory" denotes "manifested excellence." "Grace" signifies "undeserved favor," or "unmerited bounty"; and its supreme example is found in the redeeming love of God toward mankind.

How can election and foreordination be reconciled with the freedom of the human will and the moral responsibility of man? This enigma Paul does not attempt to solve. The mystery lies within the sphere of the mind and purpose of God. The human side is perfectly plain. Our duty is that of faith in Christ and of obedience to him. Paul does not mention predestination as a philosophic explanation of human life and destiny, but as a religious truth which emphasizes the reality of divine grace. He wishes to show that salvation has its origin and source in the love of God. His purpose is not speculative but intensely practical. He wishes to incite believers to seek for holiness as those who have been accepted as the sons of God. Any dealing with the problem of election must be mistaken if it intimates the possibility of that which is arbitrary or unjust. Election was in order to holiness; foreordination was to secure divine sonship. Both are according to the kind intent and loving purpose of God. When understood aright both will redound "to the praise of the glory of his grace." (Vs. 4-6a.)

As the first stanza of this hymn of praise celebrates the grace of God, the second shows this grace as manifested in Christ and in his redeeming work. This grace God "freely bestowed on us in the Beloved." It is in him and in virtue of our relation to him that we become sharers of this grace. He is called "the Beloved." Nowhere else in the New Testament does the title appear. We are prepared for it, however, by the scene at the baptism or the transfiguration when we hear the words, "This is my beloved Son." The usage of the Old Testament also reminds us that Christ in a unique sense was the Beloved of the Father. In him "we have our redemption through his blood, the forgiveness of our trespasses." Redemption denotes release secured by the payment of a ransom. The blood of Christ is declared to be the price he paid to deliver us from the penalties due for our trespasses. Christ himself indicated this when he declared that he had come "to give his life a ransom for many," or again when he said, "This [cup] is my blood of the covenant, which is poured out for many unto remission of sins."

Paul gives the first place in importance to this manifestation of God's grace. The deeper his sense of the deadliness of sin and of the holiness of God, the more will one be inclined to this view, and the more will one realize that this redemption is "according to" the limitless wealth of the unmerited favor of God, "the riches of his grace."

This redeeming grace "he made to abound toward us in all wisdom and prudence." Spiritual insight and practical intelligence and an understanding of the deep things of God are thus mentioned as gifts of grace accompanying the forgiveness of sins. This was notably true in the early church where men and women gathered from the lowest ranks of society, even slaves and freedmen, were enabled to understand such truths, for example, as are set forth in this very epistle.

The particular realities, however, to which Paul here refers are those relating to the divine counsels, specifically that of bringing unity into the entire universe through Christ, "making known unto us the mystery of his will . . . to sum up all things in Christ, the things in the heavens, and the things upon the earth."

A "mystery" means, in New Testament usage, not something which cannot be known, but something once unknown and now revealed. This revelation, made to his church, concerns the gracious plan of God concerning Christ. This plan is "according to his good pleasure which he purposed in him." It is to be realized in "a dispensation of the fulness of the times." The period here indicated extends from the First Advent of Christ until the Second. In him, as the Head of the church, all created things are to be brought into one. All are to center in him. This unity is to include all things on earth and in heaven.

It is evident, then, that Paul's view of election includes a magnificent form of universalism. However, it must be remembered that this glorious consummation is to be "in Christ" and concerns only those who accept and honor his Lordship and his Headship. The phrase points to a time when the whole creation will be brought by Christ to a condition of unity and harmony and peace.

For the service of God, and for a share in his glory at such a time, the church of Christ is destined, and is being now prepared. It is indeed the beginning of that process

by which all things are to be gathered together in Christ.
Through their union with Christ, believers have become
God's heritage. Not only has he made known to them his
purposes of bringing all things into a unity in Christ at
"the fulness of the times," but even now he has made them
his own people. They have been chosen by him to be his
special possession.

This is due to their "having been foreordained according
to the purpose of him who worketh all things after the
counsel of his will." Such a statement, referring God's
ownership in his people to his foreordaining purpose, car-
ries back the thought to the first stanza of the hymn of
praise which emphasized the divine election and foreordination and "good pleasure." The reference to the "dispensation of the fulness of the times" points to the future with
which the third stanza of the hymn is specially concerned.
This second stanza, however, comes to its close with the
refrain, "Unto the praise of his glory." This defines the
purpose of God in making us his own possession, his "heritage." It was in order that through the church the goodness and grace and love of God might be set forth, ac-
knowledged, and adored.

As Paul comes to the last stanza of his hymn of praise,
he dwells upon the blessedness of the church when God's
purposes are at last fulfilled and the redemption of the
church is complete, and believers are made partakers of the
heavenly glory of God.

Paul here introduces, however, a new thought. It is one
which is to have a prominent place in the epistle, namely,
that Gentiles as well as Jews are members of the church
and form a part of God's "heritage," and are to be joint
partakers in the glory and blessedness which believers are
yet to share.

Paul describes himself and his fellow Jewish Christians
as those "who had before hoped in Christ." The coming
of the Messiah and salvation through him had been the
hope of Israel. It was shared by all the faithful, even be-

fore Christ came. It was unknown to the Gentiles. The latter, however, have now come to hope in Christ. They have "heard the word of the truth"; they have received the good news, "the gospel," of salvation. By that gospel "the hope"—for all who trust in Christ, both Jews and Gentiles —has been enlarged and glorified and confirmed.

They have been "sealed with the Holy Spirit of promise." A seal was a sign of ownership; it was a mark of protection; it was a stamp of validity. The emphasis here is upon the fact that the gift to them of the Holy Spirit was a sign that Gentile believers, as truly as Jewish believers, belonged to the people of God, the church of Christ. This gift of the Holy Spirit, however, was further an assurance of their salvation. It was also a seal of their divine sonship.

The Holy Spirit is here designated as "the Holy Spirit of promise" because his manifestation at Pentecost and his presence with all believers had been predicted by the prophets and assured by Christ.

The Holy Spirit is further designated as "an earnest of our inheritance." Here by the use of the pronoun "our," Paul unites both Jewish and Gentile believers as sharing in the common hope. This hope looks to a future "inheritance" of glory. Of this inheritance the Holy Spirit is an "earnest." Now, an earnest was a portion of the purchase money given as the seal of a contract, and so was a pledge of full payment. It was not only a seal, however. It was an installment, a part of the price, the same in kind as the full payment. Thus the Holy Spirit, as a gift to believers, indicates the nature of the future glorified life. The essence of that life is to be spiritual, and its chief blessedness will consist in the enjoyment of spiritual perfection, and in that divine fellowship which is now made possible by the gift of the Holy Spirit.

This blessedness is at present, however, far from perfect. The sealing of the Spirit is designed to make us certain of that completed salvation which the future will bring. It leads unto "the redemption of God's own possession." For this redemption the full price has been paid, but the effects of redemption are only in part enjoyed. As Christians we are still waiting for "the redemption of our body," and for that eternal and glorious life which is to be ours as the sons of God.

The sealing of the Spirit is further designed to secure the thankful acknowledgment of the mercy and grace and love manifested by God toward the church. It is "unto the praise of his glory."

B. THE PRAYER FOR KNOWLEDGE
Ch. 1:15-23

15 For this cause I also, having heard of the faith in the Lord Jesus which is among you, and the love which ye show toward all the saints, 16 cease not to give thanks for you, making mention of you in my prayers; 17 that the God of our Lord Jesus Christ, the Father of glory, may give unto you a spirit of wisdom and revelation in the knowledge of him; 18 having the eyes of your heart enlightened, that ye may know what is the hope of his calling, what the riches of the glory of his inheritance in the saints, 19 and what the exceeding greatness of his power to us-ward who believe, according to that working of the strength of his might 20 which he wrought in Christ, when he raised him from the dead, and made him to sit at his right hand in the heavenly places, 21 far above all rule, and authority, and power, and dominion, and every name that is named, not only in this world, but also in that which is to come: 22 and he put all things in subjection under his feet, and gave him to be head over all things to the church, 23 which is his body, the fulness of him that filleth all in all.

Usually Paul opens his epistles with a thanksgiving for the spiritual graces of his readers, which is followed by a prayer for their further development and growth. He then begins his great messages of teaching and exhortation. In this epistle, however, all the truth he wishes to impart seems to be set forth in the form of praise and of prayer. The great apostle seems to instruct his readers while on his knees. The first three chapters are almost wholly occupied with expressions of gratitude and desire. The last three chapters are merely practical applications of the truths thus set forth in acts of devotion.

At least it is true that no one can tell where the opening prayer ends and the "doctrinal section" of the epistle begins. The prayer is so full of sublime teaching that many expositors stop abruptly in the midst of the sentence, and insist that the doctrinal section begins with the latter half of the nineteenth verse.

This is rather arbitrary. It is probably best to regard the introductory prayer of the epistle as comprising the whole of the majestic sentence with which the first chapter is brought to its close.

This petition is based upon the thanksgiving which it follows. Paul has set forth the spiritual blessings which have been granted in Christ. He has traced the redemption and adoption of his readers back to the foreordaining grace of God, and forward to the glorious consummation when their salvation will be complete.

It is "for this cause," and with this in view, that he offers his prayer. Yet the prayer itself begins with a note of praise. Paul expresses gratitude for the report which has reached him of the faith and love of his readers. "I also, having heard of the faith in the Lord Jesus which is among you," writes the apostle, "and the love which ye show toward all the saints, cease not to give thanks for you, making mention of you in my prayers." It is true that many ancient manuscripts omit the word "love" from this thanksgiving. In this case, however, the sense would not be greatly altered, for Paul would then seem to say that their faith rested in Christ and was manifested toward their fellow Christians; and how could it be manifested but in acts of sympathetic love? With either reading, Paul is express-

ing his grateful joy at the report of their devotion to Christ
and to his church.

In its substance the prayer is a request for knowledge,
for fuller knowledge, for an experimental knowledge of all
those divine blessings which have been set forth in the
hymn of praise and with which the epistle was begun.

The prayer is addressed to "the God of our Lord Jesus
Christ, the Father of glory." Such a description of God is
not inconsistent with the highest view of the person of his
Son. Jesus never addressed God with the words, "Our
Father," though he taught men so to pray. He did recognize his Father as his God, and he thus addressed him. He
derived his life from the Father while at the same time he
was one in the same divine being. From eternity he was
"with God"—he was God; yet God sent him into the
world, God heard him when he prayed, God exalted him,
receiving him back unto the glory which had been his before the foundation of the world. With all its mystery,
there is a sublime majesty in the title, "The God of Our
Lord Jesus Christ."

God is also addressed as "the Father of glory." This is
not merely "the glorious Father," but "the Father to whom
glory belongs," of whom glory is the characteristic feature
—the Father most glorious, the all-glorious Father. It is
to such a Being that Paul offers his petition.

He requests for his readers "a spirit of wisdom and revelation." Some understand this as a request for the gift of
the Holy Spirit. Undoubtedly the Holy Spirit is present
with all believers, and it would be as a result of his gracious
presence and power that such a spirit would be possessed
by believers. It seems more probable, however, to conclude that Paul intends here to fix the thought upon the
gift rather than upon the Giver.

The meaning is in either case practically the same. Paul
asks that these Christians may be granted that moral temper, that spiritual disposition, by which they would be able
to receive divine truth and appropriate it for their lives.

"Wisdom" may be the more general term, while "revelation" may refer more specifically to the power of receiving the "mysteries" manifested in Christ. The request seems to be that the readers may be given a wise and understanding spirit—such, indeed, as only the Holy Spirit can impart.

The sphere in which this spirit is to be exercised and nourished is in that of divine things. It is definitely in the knowledge of God—"in the knowledge of him." Human philosophy was largely contained in the maxim, "Know thyself"; Christianity finds its essence in the knowledge of God revealed in Christ: "And this is life eternal, that they should know thee the only true God, and him, whom thou didst send, even Jesus Christ."

The character of this knowledge for which Paul prays is described as being a complete and practical and experimental knowledge. He wishes that his readers may have a fuller understanding of God and his grace, and also may be able to apply this knowledge to daily life and experience.

He accordingly prays that "the eyes" of their "heart" may be "enlightened." The "heart," according to the usage of the day, was regarded as the seat, not only of the affections, but of the intellect and the will. The knowledge for which Paul asks is therefore definitely spiritual and practical. His request is for an awakened and an enlarged moral perception, for a clearer spiritual vision.

There are three objects which the apostle desires his readers more clearly, more fully, more practically, to perceive: "the hope" to which God has called them; "the riches" he possesses in them; and the "power" he is prepared to exert toward them.

The "hope of his calling" is the hope inspired by the call of God. It belongs to that call. He graciously summons us to a new life in Christ. He enables us to accept this high and holy and heavenly invitation. So in the epistles, the "called of God" are those who have obeyed his divine call and have become followers of Christ.

This call inspires and includes a confident expectation

of eternal blessedness. It is a "hope of righteousness" and of a transformation of moral character. The children of God are yet to be "conformed to the image of his Son." "If he shall be manifested, we shall be like him; for we shall see him even as he is."

It is a hope which also includes as its object the transfiguration of the body and a share in the divine glory. In this hope "were we saved," and "we rejoice in hope of the glory of God." This hope will not deceive. It is "an anchor of the soul." It is "laid up for . . . [us] in the heavens." Paul would have his readers know the essence and the content of such a call.

The second object of knowledge concerns the church of Christ. Paul prays that believers may understand how precious this church is to God. He wishes them to appreciate "the riches of the glory of his inheritance in the saints." The Christian church is the special possession of God. He has made it his heritage. It was purchased with the blood of his Son. It has been called into being by the work of his Spirit. It is to be through all eternity a proof and demonstration of his grace. Upon this church men still look with "scornful wonder." They fail to realize its origin, its influence, its eternal destiny. Members of the church, however, should appreciate their dignity. They are God's own people. They have been chosen by him to show forth his glory. They belong to that city of which the walls are of jasper, the gates are of pearl, and the streets are of gold. In the light of that city all the nations of the world are yet to rejoice.

In the third place Paul prays that we may know, in reference to God, what is "the exceeding greatness of his power to us-ward who believe." How great is that power? How much strength is available for the Christian in his daily living? How much of divine energy has God already manifested toward us? How great is that might to which we can look for the fulfillment of our hope and for the strengthening and perfecting of the church?

The resurrection and exaltation of Christ are set forth in
answer to these questions. They are at once the measure
and the illustration of what has been done, of what is being
done, of what yet is to be done in and through believers,
who together form the mystical body of Christ. The
power which God is exerting toward the church is "according to that working of the strength of his might which he
wrought in Christ, when he raised him from the dead, and
made him to sit at his right hand in the heavenly places."

This parallel and comparison are to form the very substance of the great paragraph of doctrinal instruction which
follows this prayer for knowledge. Here the intention is
practical. The apostle is urging us to depend upon this
power. He would incline us to seek this inexhaustible
source of strength. He prays that we may know fully, may
appropriate personally, and may learn in experience the
measureless might, the exceeding greatness of the power
which God is exerting "to us-ward who believe."

How much power was necessary to take Christ, crucified, mutilated, disgraced, dead, and to raise him in new-
ness of life, radiant, triumphant, glorious, and place him
at the right hand of God on his throne in heaven? That
same power is ours, if we trust in Christ, if we are members of his body, if we belong to his church. This Paul
would have us believe, and act upon the belief. Surely
this should quicken our hope, should enable us to appreciate the worth of the church, should strengthen us to
maintain against all enemies the heavenly places where we
are seated by faith in Christ Jesus.

The exaltation of Christ is depicted in terms of mysterious majesty. It is expressed in two relationships, first
toward the created universe and second toward the new
creation, his church. As to the first, Christ is declared to
be "far above all rule, and authority, and power, and dominion, and every name that is named, not only in this
world, but also in that which is to come." The terms are
supposed to refer to orders of angelic and superhuman be-

ings, as to which there was much speculation in the time
of Paul. The apostle does not intend here to give his sanc-
tion to any theory of specified orders or ranks in this unseen world. Rather he wishes to put aside all such idle
discussion but to use familiar phrases to express the unique
supremacy and absolute sovereignty of Christ. He meant
that whatever superhuman powers existed and however
they might be named, Christ was supreme over all which
now existed or might hereafter exist in any possible future.

Paul further adds, "And he put all things in subjection
under his feet." The idea is taken from the Eighth Psalm.
There was described the ideal of supremacy intended for
man but realized in Christ as the perfect representative of
all mankind as he assumed the place of universal rule and
authority at the right hand of God.

However, the relation of Christ to the church is no less
important and unique. He has been made "to be head
over all things to the church, which is his body." This
Headship of Christ over the church is a consequence of his
Headship over all things and is included in that idea. It is
in his capacity of Head over all things that he is given to
the church. The profound truth now added sets forth
more exactly the relation of Christ to the church as its exalted Head. The church is declared to be "his body."

The figure of speech which describes a society or organization of men by the picture of a human body is not original with Paul. The Greeks so conceived the political organization of the state, and had the very conception which
is contained in the phrase, "the body politic." In his letter to the Corinthians, Paul elaborated the figure of the
body with its many members to urge unity of action upon
that divided company of Christians. What is original with
Paul, and what is emphasized here, is the Headship of
Christ over the church as his body. This great idea pervades this epistle, as it does the epistle to the Colossians.
It is the characteristic conception by which these two letters are united. According to it the church is a spiritual

unity in vital relation with Christ. He brings the church into being. He is the source of its life. He supplies it with strength. He directs its activities, or employs it as his agent for the accomplishment of his purpose and work.

This profound conception is further expressed in the additional phrase which defines the church, with which the prayer comes to its close: "The fulness of him that filleth all in all." There is no question as to the difficulty of interpreting the exact meaning of the phrase. Does it mean that Christ completes the church, or that the church completes Christ? Many hold the latter view, and emphasize the truth that, as a head, Christ is not complete without his body, although, indeed, he fills that body with all things that make its life complete. This is a beautiful conception and quite in harmony with the general teaching of the epistle, which emphasizes the glory and the privileges of the church.

Probably the latter view, however, is more in harmony with the immediate context, which shows what Christ is and does to the universe and to the church, and indicates nothing that the church does for Christ. The church in this case would be "the fulness of Christ" in the sense that it receives its "fulness" from him. He imparts to it, as his body, all its life, its strength, its grace, its gifts. He who controls the universe, supplying all its needs and pervading it with his presence and power, filling "all in all," he it is who controls his church and fills and penetrates it with his life.

C. THE GIFT OF LIFE   Ch. 2:1-10

1 And you did he make alive, when ye were dead through your trespasses and sins, 2 wherein ye once walked according to the course of this world, according to the prince of the powers of the air, of the spirit that now worketh in the sons of disobedience; 3 among whom we also all once lived in the lusts of our flesh, doing the desires of the flesh and of the mind, and were by nature children of wrath, even as the rest:— 4 but God, being rich in mercy, for his great love wherewith he loved us, 5 even when we were dead through our trespasses, made us alive together with Christ (by grace have ye been saved), 6 and raised us up with him, and made us to sit with him in the heavenly places, in Christ Jesus: 7 that in the ages to come he might show the exceeding riches of his grace in kindness toward us in Christ Jesus: 8 for by grace have ye been saved through faith; and that not of yourselves, it is the gift of God; 9 not of works, that no man should glory. 10 For we are his workmanship, created in Christ Jesus for good works, which God afore prepared that we should walk in them.

In the majestic prayer with which Paul opens the epistle he has asked that his readers may be given a practical knowledge of the divine power which operates in the lives of believers. This very power, he has declared, was manifested in the resurrection and exaltation of Christ. As Paul now begins his more formal instruction, he employs the resurrection and exaltation of Christ as an illustration of what God had done for believers in raising them from a state of spiritual death, and enabling them to live with Christ in heavenly places. In setting forth this divine work he emphasizes the grace which is its source, and the holy, helpful lives in which God designs it shall result.

The transition from the prayer to the first paragraph of instruction is indicated by a change in the personal pronoun. "And you," Paul writes, designating specifically his Gentile readers, "did he make alive, when ye were dead through your trespasses and sins." There can be a state of moral and spiritual death even in the case of persons who are otherwise intensely alive. Man is a complex being. He is commonly described as a combination of "body, soul, and spirit." It is then quite possible for one to manifest the most vigorous physical and mental life, while at the same time he is spiritually dead. To be spiritually alive one must be conscious of divine realities, of faith and love toward God, of fellowship with things eternal and unseen.

The soul that is out of communion with God is spiritually dead.

This is a pathetic picture which Paul paints. It was a world of dead men, this old pagan world. Yet such is the world today, insofar as it is a world living without God. Sin has caused this spiritual death. "Ye were dead," writes the apostle, "through your trespasses and sins." It is difficult to distinguish the difference between these two terms. In its derivation the word translated "trespass" may have pointed to sin as a fall, in contrast with sin as a failure, yet as commonly employed the meaning was much the same. Both words, however, denote disobedience to God and a refusal to obey his laws. Such actions and attitudes sever the soul from fellowship with God and thus destroy spiritual life.

This state of death, however, is one of intense activity. It is described by Paul as being directed and dominated by "the world, the flesh, and the devil." These three words have a familiar sound. They form a commonplace of modern speech. However, they summarize admirably the malign influences which control those who attempt to live without God.

These Gentile converts had "once walked according to the course [or age] of this world." Yet both "age" and "world" refer to the same time and sphere. The "world" as here used by Paul refers to the present order of things as evil. The "age" describes the whole world period as transitory. The admirable translation, "course of this world," denotes a life shaped by the godless standards and aims which result in moral ruin. Already such a "course" has been defined by the apostle in speaking of those "trespasses and sins, wherein" his Gentile readers "once walked."

They had walked also "according to the prince of the powers of the air." Undoubtedly the reference is to Satan. It is, however, somewhat difficult to state the exact meaning of the words found in this clause and the next. The air

was popularly supposed to be the abode of evil spirits.
They were above the world of men and below the realm of
angels. Of these hosts or "powers," Satan is pictured as
being the prince. It is hardly necessary to conclude that
Paul sanctioned all the conceptions with which these
phrases were commonly connected. Possibly it is enough
to suppose that he is speaking figuratively to denote that
the moral atmosphere of the world, the air that men
breathe, the "spirit of the age," is vitiated by Satan and
with evil.

Satan is further defined as the prince "of the spirit that
now worketh in the sons of disobedience." "Disobedience" refers here to obstinate opposition to the divine will.
"Sons of disobedience" defines those persons of whom it
can be said that "disobedience" is the characteristic feature
of their relation to God. Their spirit is described as controlled by the same malign agency. Thus the power of
Satan is exerted, not only over the forces of evil which
dominate "the air," but also over that spirit which works
wickedly in the hearts of those who are disobedient to God.

Those who were spiritually dead, however, were controlled not only by the world and the devil, but also by the
"flesh." As Paul turns to this feature of his description he
adds that these Gentile converts had been no exception in
their moral condition. All Christians, Jews and Gentiles
alike, had once lived in sinful opposition to the will of God.
As Paul confesses, "We also all once lived in the lusts of
our flesh, doing the desires of the flesh and of the mind."
"Lusts" here denotes "the cravings," and particularly
"cravings" for what is wrong. The "flesh" signifies man's
lower nature, his physical and mental and moral being as
separated from God and controlled by sin. These cravings
arose not only from the lower nature in general, but from
its "thoughts," its perverted imaginations and memories
and habits of mind. Paul acknowledges that even in the
case of the Jews their course of life had once been determined by these desires of the flesh and of the mind. He

admits that, in spite of God's covenant and of their special privileges, they "were by nature children of wrath, even as the rest."

Thus by obeying their natural impulses, Jewish as well as Gentile believers, before they knew Christ, had incurred the divine displeasure. They were "children of wrath." In connection with such a reference to the wrath of God it is hardly necessary to note that there is not the slightest intimation of passion or revenge. Nothing is intended which is vindictive or arbitrary. The wrath of God is the obverse aspect of his love. He has established laws for the happiness of men. He has created men for fellowship with himself. Disobedience to his laws and enmity against him cannot but result in condemnation, in penalty, and in pain. The wrath of God is his holy displeasure against sin. Paul is reminding his readers that they all, whether Jews or Gentiles, were under such displeasure—they were "doomed to wrath"—when divine grace found them and gave them new life and brought them into a blessed relation to God, not merely as sinners forgiven, but as his own sons.

Paul sees no contradiction here. The holy God who hates sin loves sinners. At infinite cost he gave his own Son to redeem them. He offers them, in Christ, life and peace and participation in his eternal glory. All that they enjoy is due to the fact that he is "rich in mercy," and to "his great love wherewith he loved us."

The experience of believers is pictured in terms of the resurrection and exaltation of Christ. He was actually dead. There is no doubt of that. He was crucified, dead, and buried, and for three days his lifeless body lay in Joseph's rock-hewn tomb. So once we were dead. We were separated from holiness and purity and from God. We were held under the power of "the world, the flesh, and the devil." This spiritual death was due to the "trespasses" which Paul has already named. "We were dead through our trespasses," he here reaffirms.

Christ, however, was actually raised from the dead. For

him it was not only a spiritual experience. In the very
body which bore the prints of the spear thrust and the nails,
he appeared to his disciples. With these friends he walked
and talked and ate and drank. So, in all truth, new moral
and spiritual life is granted to believers in Christ. God has
"made us alive together with Christ . . . and raised us up
with him." Such a spiritual experience is a reality. It is
manifest by moral actions and proofs as true as those of
the empty tomb and the appearances of the risen Lord.

It is evident that this new life manifested by the Christian is yet quite imperfect. He is like Lazarus, the friend
of Jesus, who heard the divine call, and came forth from
the place of burial, "bound hand and foot with grave-
clothes." So there is much about the Christian that belongs to the dead world from which he has been delivered,
much that savors of the time when he lay helpless under
the power of sin. Yet where there is true life it is certain
to develop. We are being transformed into the image of
Christ. "If he shall be manifested, we shall be like him."

Nor yet does the physical state of the Christian now correspond to the ideal of a perfect life. Yet some day our
share in the resurrection of Christ will be manifest by the
transformation of our bodies into the likeness of the glorified body of our Lord.

Not only was Christ raised from the dead; he ascended
into heaven. He was exalted to the right hand of God. So
of believers Paul writes that God has "made us to sit with
him in the heavenly places." Our position is not regarded
as still among men who are dead in "trespasses and sins."
Nor do we belong to the region of the "air" which is dominated by powers of evil. Already, in the view of the apostle, we have entered upon a heavenly experience of fellowship with God and of life in his presence. These realms
we can and must maintain against all the forces which
would degrade us and despoil us of our treasures of peace
and holiness and joy.

The whole experience, however, is due to our relation to

Christ. It is dependent entirely upon our vital union with
him. As Paul declares of this spiritual resurrection, it is
"in Christ Jesus."

Again we are reminded that the experience is not perfected in the present, nor bound by time. It belongs to the
eternities. It is in accordance with the purpose of God,
"that in the ages to come he might show the exceeding
riches of his grace in kindness toward us in Christ Jesus."

Here Paul sounds with increased emphasis the sublime
keynote of his inspired composition. This new life with
Christ is due wholly to the unmerited favor of God. The
whole message speaks of grace issuing in life. These are
the phrases which Paul is employing, as he refers to this divine work: God is "rich in mercy"; "his great love wherewith he loved us"; "by grace have ye been saved"; "exceeding riches of his grace in kindness toward us." Thus
here he is saying, "By grace have ye been saved through
faith." Faith is the instrument by which the gift is received. It is not the source of the gift. It has no merit
in itself. The salvation is not of ourselves; it is the gift of
God. It is not the reward of merit. It is not secured by
good works, lest anyone "should glory."

Good works, nonetheless, have their supremely important place and part. They constitute the very purpose of
God in imparting to us new life. They are, however, the
fruit and result, not the root or the cause, of salvation. It
is impossible that we should be saved by our works, for we
ourselves, in our new life granted by grace, are the work of
God. "We are his workmanship." The word is not used
to glorify the skill or wisdom of God as a worker, nor to
intimate the perfection of the product. It is intended to
emphasize the fact that any good works which we may perform are to be ascribed to the grace of God. Good works
could not be manifested while we were dead. If they are
being now produced, it is because God has given us the life
which alone makes such good works possible. We who
have been raised from the dead form in reality a new crea-

tion. Surely good works should be performed by us, for we have been "created in Christ Jesus for good works."

That they should be and will be done by all Christians is absolutely certain, for they form part of the eternal plan. Such works, Paul declares, "God afore prepared that we should walk in them." He gives us new life, by faith in Christ, in order that works of holiness and purity and love should be wrought by us continually and habitually. Such works form the very sphere and element in which daily we must move. It was for this purpose God manifested his grace toward us in Christ. With this in view he "made us alive together with Christ . . . and raised us up with him, and made us to sit with him in the heavenly places, in Christ Jesus."

Herein, then, consists the supreme manifestation of God's power, not in our new life, not in our ascension to a place of supreme privilege, but in making it possible for us, through faith, to live lives of holiness, of beauty, and of service. As we seek so to live, we do well to repeat Paul's prayer and to ask that we may know in personal experience that the very power which raised Christ from the dead and exalted him to the right hand of God is being exerted toward us. Upon that power we may depend in the fulfillment of our humblest or highest duties in the family, in society, or in the church.

D. GRACE TO THE GENTILES   Ch. 2:11-22

11 Wherefore remember, that once ye, the Gentiles in the flesh, who are called Uncircumcision by that which is called Circumcision, in the flesh, made by hands; 12 that ye were at that time separate from Christ, alienated from the commonwealth of Israel, and strangers from the covenants of the promise, having no hope and without God in the world. 13 But now in Christ Jesus ye that once were far off are made nigh in the blood of Christ. 14 For he is our peace, who made both one, and brake down the middle wall of partition, 15 having abolished in his flesh the enmity,

even *the law of commandments* contained *in ordinances;*
that he might create in himself of the two one new man, so
making peace; 16 and might reconcile them both in one
body unto God through the cross, having slain the enmity
thereby: 17 and he came and preached peace to you that
were far off, and peace to them that were nigh: 18 for
through him we both have our access in one Spirit unto the
Father. 19 So then ye are no more strangers and sojourn-
ers, but ye are fellow-citizens with the saints, and of the
household of God, 20 being built upon the foundation of
the apostles and prophets, Christ Jesus himself being the
chief corner stone; 21 in whom each several building,
fitly framed together, groweth into a holy temple in the
Lord; 22 in whom ye also are builded together for a habi-
tation of God in the Spirit.

The grace of God to the church may be regarded properly as the theme of Paul's epistle to the Ephesians. However, one particular phase of this grace is emphasized. The
apostle dwells upon the mercy God has shown toward
Gentile believers. He intimates that in their reception into
the communion of his people the grace of God finds its climax and culmination. Upon this special aspect of his subject Paul now proceeds to dwell.

He reminds these Gentiles of their condition before they
learned of Christ. They were inferior to the Jews in their
religious privileges, and from the Jews they were separated by ceremonials and beliefs, by prejudice and hate.
Their state was desperate and godless. Now, however, by
the reconciling work of Christ and through faith in him,
they have been brought into fellowship with God and his
people. Now they are united with Jewish believers to form
"one new man," one body, one city, one family, one spiritual temple.

What led Paul to deal thus specifically with the relation
of Jewish and Gentile believers, one can only conjecture.
Of course Jews were found in every part of the world, as
they are today, and everywhere their relation to Gentiles
was that of mutual animosity and contempt. They formed

the nucleus of the early church and were numbered in the membership of practically all local congregations of Christians. In previous epistles Paul had to deal with the endeavor on the part of Jewish Christians to bind upon Gentile believers the yoke of their ceremonial law. On the other hand, the Gentile readers of this letter seem to have regarded themselves as superior to their Jewish brethren. At least Paul found it necessary to call to mind their former hopeless condition and, in the closing chapters of his letter, to warn them against the danger of falling back into their former pagan vices and modes of life.

Whatever may have led Paul to this phase of his discussion, all modern readers will recognize that this paragraph is of supreme present-day importance. It indicates that in Christ alone can be found the remedy for religious hatred, for race prejudice, and for class warfare.

Probably it was to glorify the grace of God that Paul thus referred to the past condition of the Gentiles. "Wherefore," writes the apostle, referring to spiritual resurrection and exaltation with Christ, "remember" what "once" you were. The contrast between their present position and the dark past will increase their gratitude to God and make them more eager to do the "good works" which God has "prepared" for them. Paul calls them "Gentiles in the flesh" to indicate that they lacked the sign and seal which guaranteed to Israel, as the people of God, his promised redemption. They were therefore called the "Uncircumcision." This term indicated their actual condition, even though it was applied to them in contempt by Jews who themselves were only in name and not in reality the people of God. These unbelieving Jews proudly called themselves the "Circumcision," while in reality they were uncircumcised in heart and mind. Their circumcision was only "in the flesh, made by hands." Between such unbelieving Jews and the unconverted Gentiles there was little difference. They were "children of wrath," just as other men, as Paul has stated in a previous verse. For them, the observances of the Mosaic law were mere empty, meaningless rites. They had no ground for despising the Gentiles or treating them with contempt.

Mere physical conditions or material possessions do not afford just grounds on which one race or nation or class can claim superiority over another. These are no proofs of moral and spiritual attainments. A ceremonial rite could not make a man a true Israelite.

Nevertheless, there were true Israelites. There were those among the Jews who really belonged to the people of God. There were those for whom outward ceremonies indicated devotion of heart and obedience to God and an assured part in his provisions of grace and love.

To this true people of God the Gentiles had not belonged. Their lack of the seal of the Jewish covenant was a correct index of their actual state. This state Paul proceeds to describe. He does so in five significant phrases. "Ye were at that time," he writes, "separate from Christ, alienated from the commonwealth of Israel, and strangers from the covenants of the promise, having no hope and without God in the world."

The first of these phrases, "separate from Christ," is possibly the most significant of all, and may include the other four. For Christ, the Messiah, the Anointed Savior, the Jews had been waiting. All hopes centered in him; by him all their expectations were to be fulfilled. The Gentiles had no relation to this Messiah. They were without a Deliverer, without a Redeemer.

So is everyone today who is separated from Christ; and as a consequence, like the Gentiles whom Paul addressed, such a one is "alienated from the commonwealth of Israel," that is, he is not "at home" with the people of God. The Gentiles had no part in that state or commonwealth of which God was the Head, and in which the will of God was the only law.

These Gentiles were "strangers from the covenants of the promise." These covenants were those made with

Abraham and the patriarchs in which redemption had been promised to their descendants. So it is true that one who is "separate from Christ" has no part in that new covenant of redemption which Christ has sealed with his own precious blood.

"Having no hope," well describes the ancient Gentile world. It also describes the world today, insofar as this world is separate from Christ. He is the only hope of the individual or of the race. Pessimism springs from unbelief. Christ is "our hope." He is the ground of our fondest expectations for time and for eternity.

The Gentiles were pictured last of all, as being "without God in the world." They had other deities. They worshiped "gods many, and lords many." Yet they were ignorant of the one living and true God. In that sense they were atheists, moving in a world alienated from God and living in ignorance of him.

Nor can those who are "separate from Christ" enjoy a saving knowledge of God. The Son reveals the Father. He is the Way, the Truth, and the Life. No one comes unto the Father but by him. It is pitifully true that the old pagan world was "without God."

From this distressing picture of what the Gentiles had been, Paul turns to describe what has been done for them by Christ. He has brought them into fellowship with God and made them one with the true people of God. "But now," says the apostle, "in Christ Jesus ye that once were far off are made nigh in the blood of Christ." Once they were "separate from Christ." Now they are living in vital union with him. Once they were excluded from the commonwealth of Israel and from the covenants of promise; they were without hope and without God. Now they belong to the true Israel, they are under a new covenant, they are inspired with immortal hopes, they are enjoying the privileges of God's own sons. All this has been accomplished for them "in the blood of Christ." All this has been secured by his atoning death. It is all the result of his redeeming work.

"He is our peace."   Not only has he made peace; he is
that peace.   It is identified with his person and work.
Aside from him, and without fellowship with him, that
peace cannot be known and enjoyed.   This is true of peace
in its widest aspects.   Particularly is this true of peace with
God, and of peace between Jew and Gentile.   It is of this
last form of peace that Paul is here speaking, namely, of
the reconciliation with God which had made possible reconciliation between the hostile races of men.

He has "made both one"—both parties, Jews and Gentiles.   He has not brought Gentiles into a society of Jews,
nor Jews into a society of Gentiles.   He has made of the
two a new unity, a new organism, a new body, in which
the old distinctions between Jews and Gentiles are forever
done away.   He "brake down the middle wall of partition,"
bringing to an end the religious and moral and social separation which had made all fellowship between Jews and
Gentiles impossible.   God had given to Israel sacred insti-
tutions designed to protect his people from the iniquities of
surrounding idolatry, but these had been abused by the
Jews as grounds for the most narrow and bitter exclusive-
ness.   The Jews had despised the Gentiles for not observ-
ing their rites and ceremonies, and the Jews were hated by
the Gentiles in return.

This hostile feeling Christ put away by his sacrificial
death.   He "abolished in his flesh the enmity."   The source
of this enmity lay in the Jewish law, which Paul describes
as "the law of commandments contained in ordinances."
This law, which was made up of commandments expressed
in decrees, had been abrogated by the atonement of Christ.
For the law, as a means of salvation, has been done away.
In a real sense "Christ is the end of the law unto righteousness to every one that believeth."   This refers to the whole
law, moral and ceremonial.   Salvation is of grace, by faith,
and not by obedience to commands and ordinances.   Faith
issues in a new life which naturally expresses itself in works
of righteousness.   The moral law retains its obligation over
Christians, not because the Jewish law was annulled only

in part, but because the obligations of morality are universal and independent of the Mosaic law. A Christian lives a moral life, not because of external ordinances, but because such a life is the inevitable result of the indwelling Spirit of Christ.

The whole Jewish law, which had been the occasion of enmity between Jew and Gentile, was abrogated by Christ, "that he might create in himself of the two one new man, so making peace." This union of Jews and Gentiles was possible only in Christ. This new creation has not made a Gentile into a Jew, nor a Jew into a Gentile, but it has transformed both into a "new man"; both have received a new nature. Thus, through a living communion with Christ, peace has been established between them.

This reconciliation between Jew and Gentile has further a larger and more significant purpose, namely, "that he . . . might reconcile them both in one body unto God." There is something very striking in the relation of these ideas as expressed by Paul. It might be supposed that Jews and Gentiles were reconciled to God that, as one of many results, they might be reconciled to each other. Paul here reverses the thought. They are reconciled to one another in order that "in one body," unitedly, they may be brought into a relation to God. This new relation is that of reconciliation which could be accomplished only "through the cross." It is the cross which makes it possible for God to accept sinful men as righteous; it is the cross which makes it possible for sinful men to approach God with confidence and trust. It is the cross, as Paul here affirms, that has "slain the enmity" between Jew and Gentile. Surely there should be no barriers of hatred and contempt between men who have been redeemed by the precious blood of Christ.

Thus the estrangement which Christ put away is both that between man and God and that between Gentile and Jew. As a result of his reconciling work Christ, by his Spirit, and through his apostles and prophets, "came and preached peace"—peace both to the Gentiles, who had

been "far off" from the people of God, and "to them that
were nigh," that is, to the Jews who as a nation were in a
special relation to God.

The proof that peace has been made by Christ and proclaimed by Christ, and accepted by both Jews and Gentiles, is given in the arresting statement, "For through him
we both have our access in one Spirit unto the Father."
Here the relation of believers to the three Persons in the
adorable Trinity is stated in three comprehensive phrases:
"through" the Son; "in" the Spirit; "unto" the Father.
Their new relation to God, their reconciliation to God,
their peace with God are all due to the atoning work of the
Son, "in . . . [his] blood," "in his flesh," through his
cross. This new relation is "in the Spirit," that is, by his
influence and power, as of persons who have been born of
the Spirit, who are led by the Spirit, who are filled by
the Spirit, and who realize the unity of the Spirit.

This new relation is pictured as an "access," or introduction, or right of approach. We are brought to God
through Christ, in the Spirit, and have the right to approach him as our Father. Here is thus a clear affirmation of our "sonship," or adoption. As Christians we at
all times have the privilege of access to God as sons to a
loving Father.

Therefore, as a result of this reconciliation and in view
of the atoning work of Christ, Jews and Gentiles are united
in the one body of Christ, namely, his church. This union
Paul pictures by a number of swiftly changing figures of
speech. Gentile and Jewish believers together form one
commonwealth, one family, one building, one temple.

"So then," as a result of the salvation in which you alike
partake, "ye are no more strangers and sojourners."
"Strangers" described foreigners in general, persons belonging to another country; "sojourners" defined foreigners dwelling in a land for a time but not having the rights
of citizens. Such had been the condition of these Gentiles.

Now, however, because of redemption and adoption,

"Ye are fellow-citizens with the saints." Here, as is usual with Paul, "saints" denotes Christians in general, the whole body of believers. To this body the Gentile Christians belong. Together with Jewish believers they form the true Israel of God; they are the seed of Abraham.

Therefore Paul adds that they are now "of the household of God"; they belong to his house or family. Furthermore, the idea of a house suggests a building. So, further to express their spiritual unity with Jewish believers, Paul declares that these Gentiles, by their faith in Christ, are being built into a great structure upon "the foundation of the apostles and prophets, Christ Jesus himself being the chief corner stone."

The prophets here mentioned are not those of the Old Testament, but of the New. They refer to those men who were gifted by the Holy Spirit as the inspired teachers of the Christian gospel. It is difficult to decide whether these apostles and prophets are regarded as the foundation of the church or whether the doctrines which they taught formed such a foundation. Does Paul mean "the foundation" which consisted of "apostles and prophets" or the foundation which apostles and prophets laid? Both ideas are true. It seems, however, more in harmony with the whole paragraph to conclude that, as Paul is here speaking of persons and not of doctrines, he means that the foundation was composed of the apostles and prophets, as the superstructure is composed of all other believers who by faith are united to Christ. This picture of the foundation finds a parallel in the description of the New Jerusalem, of which it is said, "The wall of the city had twelve foundations, and on them twelve names of the twelve apostles of the Lamb."

Into this glorious structure of living stones Gentile and Jewish believers alike were being built, "Christ Jesus himself being the chief corner stone." It is he who supports and holds together both the foundation and the walls. It is faith in him which gives to every believer a place in the building, and it is Christ who gives to the structure its unity and its strength.

In him "each several building, fitly framed together, groweth into a holy temple in the Lord." The picture is that of a great structure with one harmonious design. Every constituent part is being adjusted to the whole and the entire edifice is being brought to completion. Here the design is that of a glorious temple. Its beauty and holiness are due to the fact that every part has a vital relation to Christ. The Gentile Christians to whom the epistle is addressed are thus assured that they have a place in this building. They once were without "hope and without God in the world." Now they are united with Christ. Therefore they, too, as well as Jewish believers, "are builded together for a habitation of God in the Spirit."

As Paul here describes the church under the figure of a temple, some suppose that he had in mind the temple of Diana, which was the pride of Ephesus and one of the Seven Wonders of the World. Others suppose that he was thinking of the Temple at Jerusalem. However, all realize how infinitely the real temple surpasses any building made by hands. Its massive foundation and glorious walls are composed of living souls. Every believer who is united with Christ by a vital faith has a place in this structure. It thus includes men of all races and times. This sanctuary God has made to be his dwelling place. Someday the building will be complete and will become a source of blessing and rejoicing to the whole world.

E. THE MESSENGER OF GRACE   Ch. 3:1-13

1 For this cause I Paul, the prisoner of Christ Jesus in behalf of you Gentiles,—2 if so be that ye have heard of the dispensation of that grace of God which was given me to you-ward; 3 how that by revelation was made known unto me the mystery, as I wrote before in few words, 4 whereby, when ye read, ye can perceive my understand-

*ing in the mystery of Christ; 5 which in other generations
was not made known unto the sons of men, as it hath now
been revealed unto his holy apostles and prophets in the
Spirit; 6 to wit, that the Gentiles are fellow-heirs, and fellow-members of the body, and fellow-partakers of the promise in Christ Jesus through the gospel, 7 whereof I was
made a minister, according to the gift of that grace of God
which was given me according to the working of his power.
8 Unto me, who am less than the least of all saints, was
this grace given, to preach unto the Gentiles the unsearchable riches of Christ; 9 and to make all men see what is
the dispensation of the mystery which for ages hath been
hid in God who created all things; 10 to the intent that
now unto the principalities and the powers in the heavenly
places might be made known through the church the manifold wisdom of God, 11 according to the eternal purpose
which he purposed in Christ Jesus our Lord: 12 in whom
we have boldness and access in confidence through our faith
in him. 13 Wherefore I ask that ye may not faint at my
tribulations for you, which are your glory.*

Paul has emphasized the grace of God to Gentile believers in that they share with believing Jews the salvation
wrought out by Christ, and he has shown that they are
being built together into a spiritual temple for the indwelling of God. With this in mind he is about to pray for
these readers, and to make his prayer the more impressive
he begins by a reference to the fact that he is the chosen
apostle to the Gentiles. "For this cause," he writes, "I
Paul, the prisoner of Christ Jesus in behalf of you Gentiles"—but at the mention of his appointed ministry he
pauses to dwell upon its nature and significance, and not
until the fourteenth verse of the chapter does he resume his
prayer.

This paragraph, however, is not to be regarded as a mere
parenthesis. It is not a digression. It enlarges upon the
theme of the epistle which is the grace of God, and particularly his grace shown toward the Gentiles. In this paragraph Paul sets forth the unique character of his mission.

He is the chosen messenger of God, appointed to make known to the nations of the world the great truth that salvation in Christ has been designed from eternity for all nations as truly as for Jews. It is his unmerited privilege to declare that Gentile and Jewish believers alike are on a perfect equality as members of the church by which is being revealed, to angels as well as to men, "the manifold wisdom of God."

Paul here calls himself "the prisoner of Christ," not merely as one who is suffering in the service of Christ, but as one who belongs to Christ and whose suffering is part of the lot assigned by Christ. He is a prisoner, however, "in behalf of you Gentiles." It was because he had publicly proclaimed that the gospel was intended for all the world and that God had sent him to the Gentiles that Paul was detested by the Jews and persecuted by them. To this hatred and persecution, indeed, his present imprisonment was due.

However, in a larger sense still he was a "prisoner . . . in behalf of . . . [the] Gentiles." This imprisonment was but an incident of his career which had been peculiar in that while himself a Jew he had been proclaiming the gospel to Gentiles throughout the whole empire, beginning at Jerusalem and continuing as far as Rome.

Of this great and glorious mission his readers were well aware. "If so be that ye have heard of the dispensation of that grace of God which was given me to you-ward," he writes. Not that there was any doubt that they were well aware of the source and character of Paul's mission. This was merely a polite way of reminding them of a fact upon which he wished further to dwell even though it was quite familiar to his readers. He wished to emphasize and glorify this fact. His readers knew that he had been chosen and prepared for his mission by a gift of God's grace, designed for their benefit. They had heard of "the dispensation" or arrangement made with respect to this gift, namely, that it was by way of a direct revelation that Paul had been given a knowledge of the truth that Gentiles were admitted to all the blessings of salvation on a perfect equality with the Jews. This truth he calls a "mystery," not something which cannot be known or something difficult to understand, but something once hidden and now revealed, something, graciously communicated by God. In preparation for his mission such a divine disclosure had been made to Paul: "By revelation was made known unto me the mystery."

To this "mystery" the apostle had referred in the previous portion of his epistle. "As I wrote before in few words," he says, "whereby, when ye read, ye can perceive my understanding in the mystery of Christ." This last word sets forth the essential character and supreme content of the mystery. It is "the mystery of Christ." It concerns Christ. It centers in Christ. Paul insists that to prepare him for the ministry he has been given a supernatural revelation in reference to Christ. He will go on to explain that the content of this revelation was the fact of the equality of Gentile and Jew in all that Christ had secured.

First, however, he reminds his readers that this truth has not been clearly understood in other ages. This mystery "in other generations was not made known unto the sons of men, as it hath now been revealed." No doubt men of former times did have some knowledge of this truth. Many of the Old Testament prophets distinctly foretold the salvation of Gentiles. At the council in Jerusalem, James insisted that the Jewish Scriptures were in accord with the contention of Peter and Paul, namely, that Gentiles could be saved without keeping the Mosaic law. However, in Old Testament times it was commonly supposed that Gentiles would be saved, but that they first must become Jews in order to receive the benefits the Messiah would bring.

Now, however, God had given a fuller revelation "unto his holy apostles and prophets in the Spirit." These were the "apostles" of Christ, and the "prophets" of New Testament times. They saw most distinctly the universal love

of God. Guided and illumined by his Spirit they understood "the mystery," namely, "that the Gentiles are fellow-heirs, and fellow-members of the body, and fellow-
partakers of the promise in Christ Jesus through the
gospel."

Gentiles are "fellow-heirs." All that belonged to the
Jews as the people of God, now belongs to Gentile believers; all the glory of the future, including "the inheritance
of the saints in light," and the redemption of the body—
all this is the heritage of Gentiles and Jews alike. They
are "fellow-members of the body," standing on a perfect
equality in the church of Christ; in that body distinctions
between Jew and Gentile no longer exist; all are one in
Christ Jesus. They are "fellow-partakers of the promise"
of salvation spoken by the mouth of Jewish prophets, the
promise which God fulfilled in the gift of his Son.

Gentile believers are thus fellow heirs, fellow members,
fellow partakers, because of their relation to Christ. All
that they enjoy is through his Person and work and because they are united with him; it is all "in Christ Jesus."
It is also "through the gospel." This was the means by
which these blessings had been communicated to the Gentiles. It was indeed "good news" which had brought to
the heathen world the offer of such a salvation for all mankind.

Of this gospel Paul declares he "was made a minister."
This was a very extraordinary fact. Paul had not believed
this gospel. He had persecuted the followers of Christ.
He had despised the Gentiles. That he should have become an apostle of Christ, and should have been sent as
the chosen messenger to the Gentile world, was indeed a
marvel. It could be explained only by the unmerited kindness of God, as a "gift of that grace of God." It could be
accounted for only by "the working of his power," that divine power which suddenly transformed a persecutor into
an apostle.

Paul was not the only one to whom God revealed "the

mystery" of the perfect equality of believing Gentile and
Jew. He was not the only one who understood that the
gospel was for the whole world. The wonder was that one
so opposed to Christ, so undeserving of the grace of God,
should have been chosen as the messenger of God. Thus
Paul continues, "Unto me, who am less than the least of
all saints, was this grace given, to preach unto the Gentiles
the unsearchable riches of Christ."

Not always did Paul seem to show such humility. He
found it necessary at times to boast, and to insist that he
was "not a whit behind the very chiefest apostles." Yet
such an attitude was taken only in defense of his apostolic
authority. This authority had been given him directly
from heaven, and the most ardent defense of his divine
mission was in perfect harmony with his humblest confession of personal unworthiness. He did not deserve to be a
Christian, much less an apostle. It was when he remembered his cruelty to the followers of Christ that he con-
fessed himself not only "less than the least of all saints,"
but even the chief of sinners.

Here, however, it was his vision of the divine glory of
the gospel that made him conscious of his own unworthiness, and in this epistle which so magnifies the grace of
God, and particularly the grace of God toward Gentile believers, it is fitting that Paul should thus emphasize the
grace of God toward the messenger who was specially commissioned to proclaim the gospel of grace to the Gentile
world. He was "less than the least of all saints." The
word "saints" here means Christians in general. It does
not denote any group possessing special holiness or sanctity. It was the common designation of believers. Paul
is thus referring to himself as less worthy than "the least of
all" the followers of Christ. Undeserving as he was, however, to him "was this grace given, to preach unto the
Gentiles the unsearchable riches of Christ." The Person
of Christ, his saving work, his redeeming grace, constitute
riches which are "unsearchable," or, as some like to trans-

late the word, "inexhaustible." New treasures are ever
being discovered, but inconceivable stores lie deeper still,
and even eternity will not suffice to penetrate to the lowest
depths or to measure the infinite greatness of all that wealth
of wisdom and knowledge, of beauty and power, of sympathy and love, that are in Christ Jesus our Lord. Yet, insofar as discovered, they are always ours. They are for
our advantage. Upon them we are to draw. It is an infinite store which none can exhaust. To proclaim these
"riches of Christ" Paul was sent to the Gentile world.

Further it was Paul's mission "to make all men see what
is the dispensation of the mystery which for ages hath been
hid in God who created all things." This spiritual enlightenment he gave when he preached the gospel, and particularly when he preached the gospel to Gentile and Jew
alike, and when he insisted that both Gentile and Jew were
included in the saving purpose of God.

That the gospel of Christ was intended for the whole
world is no new idea. That Jew and Gentile are alike in
need of salvation, that both find that salvation in Christ,
and that both are united in one body by faith in Christ
are not novel conceptions. This "mystery," formerly so
imperfectly understood, has always been in the mind of
God. The evangelization of the world is no modern proj-
ect. It formed a part of the divine plan when God created the universe. Had it not been a part of that plan the
world could never attain its divine purpose and goal. Man
has been slow to understand the purpose of God. The
Jews, to whom God gave his divine revelation, narrowly
concluded that salvation was for themselves, and possibly
for some Gentiles who might ally themselves with them.
However, when redemption had been accomplished, God
opened the eyes of Paul, and others of his apostles and
prophets, to understand the wideness of his mercy and to
see that Christ had come as the Savior of the whole world.
Paul had been sent to give to all whom he might reach a
vision of this gracious, eternal purpose of God.

This ministry of Paul had even a wider outlook. The final effect of his mission was not upon men, but upon angels. It was "to the intent that now unto the principalities and the powers in the heavenly places might be made known through the church the manifold wisdom of God."

The church, brought into being by the preaching of Paul and his successors; the church in which men of all nations and tribes stand on an equality; the church in which all believers are united in one body; the true church, composed of "saints," of those who belong to God and live for God—this church of Christ is designed to be an object of wonder and amazement to heavenly beings of every station and rank. It is intended to make them realize "the manifold wisdom of God." He never is found lacking in ways and means to carry out his designs of grace and love.

All this was part of a divine plan. It was "according to the eternal purpose which he purposed in Christ Jesus our Lord." In the redemption which God planned and provided by Christ, God never designed that only one race should partake. It was for the whole world, and when proclaimed to the whole world, and when resulting in a perfected and glorious church, it would manifest the eternal purpose of God which is being fulfilled in Christ. It is in him "we have boldness and access in confidence through our faith." While indeed celestial beings may be lost in wonder at the infinite wisdom of God, yet we mortals, in spite of our limitations and frailties, need have no fear in the presence of God. We draw near to him in prayer, as the apostle is about to do, for we come in the name of Christ. Our trust is in him. In him we have "boldness," or freedom of spirit; "access" as children approaching a loving Father; and "confidence," not only in the act of prayer, but in all the experiences of life. This is possible only as "our faith" is in the Lord Jesus Christ. This is our privilege as those who belong to the one body of believers, who have been commissioned to make our Savior known to all the nations of the world.

Because the mission of the Christian apostle is so great, because he is carrying out a divine purpose which is so sublime, Paul can add, "Wherefore I ask that you may not faint at my tribulations for you, which are your glory."

Paul's readers might have lost heart. They might have supposed that the cause of Christ was failing. Their great friend and apostle was a prisoner in Rome. His work seemed to have ended. The world was not evangelized. The church was weak and imperfect. Its predicted destiny was unfulfilled. The Gentile believers might well have been discouraged.

The apostle reasoned otherwise. He was indeed suffering, and suffering for their sake. However, his painful imprisonment and distress must argue a great cause; they must signify an enterprise worthy of such a price. Paul was an apostle of Christ. Unless some great purpose was being accomplished the Master would not allow his servant to suffer such pain. Paul was performing his part in a plan formed by God before the foundation of the world, namely, the founding of the Christian church and the evangelizing of the nations of the earth. His readers should, therefore, realize that the anguish the apostle endured was in reality an honor to them. It indicated the dignity of their position, the exalted character of their destiny, which was being secured at so great a cost.

That the tribulations of Paul should be a glory to these Gentile Christians is therefore a paradox. It does not mean what it might seem to denote. They were not glad that he was suffering. However, they could feel honored that one who was accomplishing so divine a mission was suffering for them. They, too, were thus clearly given a part and a place in the benefits graciously provided in the loving purpose of God. Such a view of Paul's imprisonment should bring them encouragement and hope rather than grief and despair.

Suffering is ever involved in the enterprise of evangeliz-

ing the world. So it is in all great causes. The most priceless possessions of mankind have ever been secured by
peril, toil, and pain. The recipients of such benefits, however, realize more fully the greatness of their blessings
when they consider the sacrifice of life and treasure by
which these have been purchased. Opposition, difficulty,
even apparent failure, are not reasons for abandoning a
divinely appointed task. One needs only to be certain
that his is a work which God has projected. Then, in
furthering a divine plan, even tribulation may be a cause
and ground for glory and for praise.

F. THE PRAYER FOR SPIRITUAL POWER
Ch. 3:14-19

*14 For this cause I bow my knees unto the Father, 15
from whom every family in heaven and on earth is named,
16 that he would grant you, according to the riches of his
glory, that ye may be strengthened with power through his
Spirit in the inward man; 17 that Christ may dwell in your
hearts through faith; to the end that ye, being rooted and
grounded in love, 18 may be strong to apprehend with all
the saints what is the breadth and length and height and
depth, 19 and to know the love of Christ which passeth
knowledge, that ye may be filled unto all the fulness of God.*

The prayers of Paul are among the most precious por-
tions of the inspired Word. Quite commonly a petition for
his readers is found at the opening of an epistle. In the
case of this Ephesian letter such a request for spiritual
knowledge forms part of the introduction. However, as
that prayer summarizes much of the truth which the letter
was designed to express, so when this truth has been set
forth more fully, the doctrinal portion of the epistle is
closed with a majestic petition. In it Paul requests for his
readers spiritual strength, that Christ may dwell in their
hearts, that the love of Christ may be fully known by them,

and that the virtues and perfections of Christ may be imparted to them.

This prayer refers back to the great realities Paul has been presenting, and resumes the broken sentence with which the chapter began. "For this cause," cries the apostle—that is, in view of the grace which has imparted new life to his Gentile readers, united them with Jewish believers in one body, and built them into the living temple which is being erected for the indwelling of God—in view of such grace the apostle prays that this divine indwelling may result in a fuller knowledge and in a deepening spiritual experience of the presence and love of Christ.

"I bow my knees," he writes, to express the earnestness of his petition. Standing was the more usual posture in prayer. Kneeling is not necessary. However, the very attitude of the body and the closing of the eyes may make the experience of communion with God more real and the action of the mind more intense and alert.

Paul directs his prayer to "the Father, from whom every family in heaven and on earth is named." Christ taught his followers to address God as their Father. Such a conscious relationship to him gives confidence in prayer. Such a relation has been emphasized in this epistle. In the first chapter we were reminded of "God our Father" and were told of our "adoption as sons." In the second chapter we read of "our access in one Spirit unto the Father." Also in the third chapter Paul has written of our "boldness and access in confidence" through faith in Christ.

However, further encouragement in prayer is given by the extraordinary expression, "The Father, from whom every family in heaven and on earth is named." This is intended to describe the universal Fatherhood of God. Surely it does not suggest that "every family" is godly or that every household holds the name of God in reverence. Paul plays upon the word $\pi\alpha\tau\acute{\eta}\rho$, "father," from which the word translated "family" is formed. He means that every group or community of intelligent beings, whether of men or angels, gets the significant name of "family" from the one "Father." Each group or order is related to God as the common Father of all. Because of this relation it is given the name of family.

The universal Fatherhood is not to be forgotten. Yet it is not to be confused with that special spiritual relationship into which the redeemed are brought, by faith, when they are adopted as the sons of God. What is here described is the relation to God the Creator which is possessed by all communities and nations and orders of beings. The fact that any such community bears the significant name of family indicates that it sustains a relation to God as its Father. The readers of the epistle, both Jews and Gentiles, form one such family, of which God is the Father. This fact gives encouragement in prayer, and ground for expecting that requests will be fulfilled.

Paul asks that God may fulfill the following requests "according to the riches of his glory." The glory of God is his manifested excellence. This revelation of grace and love has found its completion in the person and work of Christ. Paul's request is that the gift for which he prays may be granted to his readers in accordance with the divine perfection which has been revealed in its glorious fullness and boundless wealth.

The prayer is specifically for spiritual strength, "that ye may be strengthened with power through his Spirit in the inward man." The source of this strength is the Holy Spirit, who is to communicate the desired power. The sphere in which it is to be realized and experienced is "the inward man," that is, in the innermost recesses of the being. The church was being built "for a habitation of God in the Spirit." Yet, what is true of the church is true of each member of the church. Each one is a temple of the Holy Spirit who dwells within. This indwelling Spirit of God is an abiding presence with every believer, but there is need of a larger and fuller manifestation of his power. All Christians need to pray for that inner quickening and enrichment for which Paul here asks, and which is made possible by the operation of the Spirit.

Identical with this indwelling and power of the Holy Spirit is the abiding presence of Christ. Thus the apostle prays "that Christ may dwell in your hearts through faith." It is the very office and function of the Spirit to make Christ real and regnant in the life of believers. "He shall glorify me" was the significant promise of the Master. What Paul here asks is that Christ may more truly take possession of these Christian readers; "that Christ may dwell in your hearts" denotes a permanent residence, an abiding presence. The heart was considered the seat of the affections, but also of the intelligence and the will. The petition is that Christ may possess the entire being, purifying the affections, enlightening the understanding, controlling the will.

Of such an indwelling, faith is the sole condition. The door of the heart must be opened. Christ is willing and ready to enter in and to become the abiding Guest, the unfailing Friend, the Giver of life, the loving Lord.

This is the very substance of the prayer. All that follows must be an unfailing result; and all is in accord with the uniform teaching of Scripture. All the desired blessings are from the Father; all are through the Son; all are by the Spirit.

Accordingly Paul's further prayer is that his readers may know fully the love of Christ for them. As a condition for such knowledge they must be themselves "rooted and grounded in love." Taken in their literal sense, these words "rooted and grounded" may be regarded as forming a mixed metaphor. By many they are so criticized. It is quite probable, however, that Paul did not intend that his readers should think specifically of either a root or a foundation. He seems rather to have used the words in their applied sense of being securely settled, and deeply founded. Love is the element in which Christians are to be thus thoroughly grounded. This "love" does not mean love for

Christ or the love of Christ, but love in general, the Christian grace of love. This grace will result from the indwelling presence of Christ, and it is indeed the fruit of the Spirit. One must be thoroughly established in love if he is fully to understand the love of Christ. It must not be a mere passing emotion, not a weak sentiment. It must be an abiding principle of life. It must be the very element in which one lives. It must be the spring and basis of all action and thought. One must needs be "rooted and grounded in love" if he is to be "strong to apprehend with all the saints what is the breadth and length and height and depth, and to know the love of Christ which passeth knowledge."

The word translated "may be strong" is different from the term "strengthened" which Paul uses above. It denotes ability or capacity. Paul prays that his readers may have the mental capacity, or may be fully able to "apprehend" or to understand the love of Christ. This spiritual understanding is not to be an individual experience, nor a peculiar endowment, but a knowledge shared by the whole community of believers. Their gift of spiritual discernment is to be enjoyed "with all the saints." To these fellow believers they are united by love and in union with them they can perceive the love of Christ in its full extent.

To indicate the vastness of this love, Paul speaks of its "breadth and length and height and depth." It is hardly wise to attempt to find a specific meaning in each one of these dimensions. Some have ventured to suggest that its breadth includes Gentile and Jew; its length is from eternity; its height is measured by the heavenly places to which it brings us; its depth, by the death Christ endured for our redemption. Such fanciful interpretations are attractive to some minds, but they hardly fall within the realm of sober exposition. Paul had quite the opposite conception in mind. Instead of offering specific measurements, he meant to indicate a love which is beyond all description and estimate; it "passeth knowledge." He had spoken of the vastness of this love of Christ for us, and he reaches his climax by asserting that it is too vast to be comprehended. What he means to pray for is that his readers may have a knowledge of Christ's love which is actual and real; that they may be so spiritually strengthened that this knowledge may grow from more to more; and that it may be a conscious blessed experience which is shared with our fellow Christians, even though a complete and exhaustive knowledge of divine love ever must be beyond the capacity of the human mind.

Yet this increasing knowledge of the love of Christ is not the ultimate blessing for which Paul prays. The end in view and his final petition for these readers is that they "may be filled unto all the fulness of God."

"The fulness of God" denotes the sum total of all his divine excellencies and perfections. The divine attributes, such as omniscience and omnipresence and omnipotence, cannot be communicated to men. Nor can men be "partakers of the divine nature" in such a way that the divine essence can be communicated to them. With the virtues of God, however, men can be increasingly filled. These virtues are all embodied in Jesus Christ. As he dwells in their hearts by faith, these graces are increasingly communicated to believers and manifested in them. The church has already been called "the fulness" of Christ, as being the body to which he is communicating his grace and which he is filling with his moral qualities. Here the apostle ventures to pray that this filling may be continued up to the full measure possessed by God. It is evident that Paul is thus putting before us an ideal which never can be attained in the present life. A nearer and nearer approach to that ideal can be made. Even though it is gradual, it should be continuous. Paul elsewhere describes the same reality under a slightly different figure, "We all, with unveiled face beholding as in a mirror the glory of the Lord, are transformed into the same image from glory to glory." The process will someday be complete: "If he shall be manifested, we shall be like him; for we shall see him even as he is."

We need to be strengthened by the Spirit, for then the presence of Christ will abide in our hearts. Then we shall know increasingly the love of Christ. Then we shall be filled with the moral excellencies of Christ even up to the divine and perfect measure. Such is the prayer of the apostle, and it should awaken an echo in the soul of every professed follower of Christ.

G. THE DOXOLOGY   Ch. 3:20-21

20 Now unto him that is able to do exceeding abundantly above all that we ask or think, according to the power that worketh in us, 21 unto him be the glory in the church and in Christ Jesus unto all generations for ever and ever. Amen.

It is no wonder that there rises from the heart of Paul such an anthem of praise. He has been dwelling in three luminous chapters upon the wondrous things wrought for the church by the grace of God, upon the still greater marvels which the future has in store, and upon the measureless excellencies God will have the church attain. However, this doxology is immediately connected with the prayer which precedes. That prayer was almost startling in its boldness. It requested that believers might attain a moral perfection akin to that possessed by God himself. This doxology begins with a statement which indicates that even such a prayer can hardly be too bold and aspiring. Paul ascribes praise "unto him that is able to do exceeding abundantly above all that we ask or think." Taken literally, two conceptions of the power of God appear to be here combined. First, God is able to do "beyond all things," that is to say, there is no limit to his power. Secondly, he is able to do superabundantly beyond the utmost we can ask or think of asking. Probably the translators are wise, however, in placing the stress upon the latter idea. Paul evidently wishes to say that while his prayer has been bold in requesting the knowledge of a love which surpasses knowledge and a moral attainment which is beyond human experience, yet he is justified in such boldness, for God is able to do superabundantly above all we can ask in prayer or can venture to conceive.

Does Paul not definitely imply that God both can and will give incredible answers to our requests for moral progress and likeness to himself? Is not this note of praise also a cry of assurance? The apostle seems to say that we cannot ask too much, and that God's giving will far surpass our boldest and loftiest request.

This assurance is strengthened by the evidence of God's grace already manifest in the lives of believers. His Spirit is already operating in them. This "power that worketh in us" is the measure and means of the limitless ability of God to do for us and in us far more than we ask or can conceive. In some such sense Paul has previously declared that the Holy Spirit is the "earnest of our inheritance." That divine power, that omnipotent Person, has already delivered these Gentile readers from the dominion of the world and the flesh and the devil. He has imparted to them new life; he has exalted them to "heavenly places in Christ." Surely then his work will be continued, and its ultimate completion can be nothing less than divine perfection. God is able to do "exceeding abundantly" for us because his ability is "according to the power that worketh in us," namely, the power of his indwelling Spirit.

"Unto him," who has done, who is doing, who will do for us more than we dare ask and more than we can conceive—"unto him" Paul ascribes "glory in the church and in Christ Jesus." As this is a doxology, Paul means to say, "Let there be glory to God." Glory is manifested excellence. Therefore the cry is this, "Let the virtues, the grace, the power, the goodness of God be manifested in the church and in Christ." Such is the possibility, the duty, the high privilege of the church. In its services of praise, in the pure lives of its members, in its worldwide proclamation of the gospel, in its ministries to human distress and need, in its heavenly destiny, the power and holiness and love of God are being made known.

However, it is in Christ Jesus, and in the church only because of its relation to Christ Jesus, that God is most truly glorified. Christ is the "brightness" of his Father's glory, "the express image of his person" (King James Version). "The only begotten Son, who is in the bosom of the Father, he hath declared him." Thus it is "in the church and in Christ Jesus" that the apostle would have God to be praised and his glory to be manifested.

Moreover this is to be "unto all generations for ever and ever." In such a phrase the apostle endeavors to express the idea of eternity. More literally the words may be translated, "Unto all the generations of the age of the ages," as if Paul were saying that each generation of that age, which includes all the ages, would add its own chorus to that great oratorio of praise with which eternity is filled. "Amen," "so let it be," writes the apostle, using a word of solemn affirmation, familiar to Old Testament readers, which from earliest times has been used in the Christian church.

With this majestic paean of praise the doctrinal portion of the epistle, chapters one to three, is brought to its close.

III
EXHORTATIONS TO THE
RECIPIENTS OF GRACE
Chs. 4:1 to 6:20

A. EXHORTATIONS TO CHRISTIAN UNITY
Ch. 4:1-16

1 I therefore, the prisoner in the Lord, beseech you to walk worthily of the calling wherewith ye were called, 2 with all lowliness and meekness, with longsuffering, forbearing one another in love; 3 giving diligence to keep the unity of the Spirit in the bond of peace. 4 There is one body, and one Spirit, even as also ye were called in one hope of your calling; 5 one Lord, one faith, one baptism, 6 one God and Father of all, who is over all, and through all, and in all. 7 But unto each one of us was the grace given according to the measure of the gift of Christ. 8 Wherefore he saith,

When he ascended on high, he led captivity captive,
And gave gifts unto men.

9 (Now this, He ascended, what is it but that he also descended into the lower parts of the earth? 10 He that descended is the same also that ascended far above all the heavens, that he might fill all things.) 11 And he gave some to be apostles; and some, prophets; and some, evangelists; and some, pastors and teachers; 12 for the perfecting of the saints, unto the work of ministering, unto the building up of the body of Christ: 13 till we all attain unto the unity of the faith, and of the knowledge of the Son of God, unto a fullgrown man, unto the measure of the stature of the fulness of Christ: 14 that we may be no longer children, tossed to and fro and carried about with every wind of doctrine, by the sleight of men, in craftiness, after the wiles of error; 15 but speaking truth in love, may grow up in all things into him, who is the head, even Christ;

16 from whom all the body fitly framed and knit together through that which every joint supplieth, according to the working in due measure of each several part, maketh the increase of the body unto the building up of itself in love.

Instruction is followed by exhortation. Such is the usual method in the epistles by Paul. Thus in this letter to the Ephesians the great doctrines are set forth in the three opening chapters, and in the last three these doctrines are applied to life. However, these divisions are not to be too closely drawn. The doctrinal section is full of practical implications, and in the practical section the duties are enforced by reference to revealed truths.

"I therefore, the prisoner in the Lord, beseech you to walk worthily of the calling wherewith ye were called," writes the apostle as he enters upon his long series of practical exhortations. "Therefore" means in view of the grace revealed in Christ, in view of the new life imparted, in view of the union of Gentiles and Jews in the church of Christ. The "therefore" is characteristic of the apostle. According to Paul, duties are always based upon doctrines, creed determines character, belief is expressed in life.

He calls himself "the prisoner in the Lord." This is not so much to arouse pity as to express his conscious dignity and his conception of the importance of the doctrines he has taught and of the instruction he is about to give. His imprisonment is in a great cause. It is being endured for the sake of Christ, and by an ambassador of Christ. As such, he beseeches or exhorts his readers to "walk worthily of the calling wherewith" they were "called." This calling has been set forth in the chapters which precede. It was the summons of the Holy Spirit to partake of the grace of God, to enjoy a place in the Christian brotherhood, to reveal the virtues of Christ, to make known his gospel in the whole world, and to share his eternal glory.

Recipients of such mercies should manifest conduct consistent with such high priveleges. They should "walk worthily" of their calling. The term "walk" is a familiar, almost a trite, figure of speech, yet it should not be allowed to lose its meaning. It defines a course of life, yet life in its more usual and customary aspects and experiences. It is the picture of one who is advancing step by step. It reminds us of the common round and the daily task. It assures us that every sphere of life gives one ample opportunity to serve his Lord and to walk worthily of his Christian calling.

Paul dwells upon life in four different spheres, or under four aspects, and he emphasizes one phase of duty in relation to each. He exhorts believers to promote unity as members of the church, to live in purity as members of society, to manifest love as members of the household, and, as Christian warriors, to put on the whole armor which God provides.

First of all, then, as members of the church, they are exhorted to "keep the unity of the Spirit in the bond of peace." To this end they are to walk "with all lowliness and meekness." Neither of these traits was highly regarded as a virtue by the pagan world. Christianity has glorified both. The former term translates a word which indicated little more than weakness; as a Christian virtue it denotes that humility which springs from a true estimate of one's own unworthiness. "Meekness" means more than mere modesty, as contrasted with "harshness." It signifies both a trustful submission to God and a consequent gentleness and self-constraint in meeting the provocations of others. It is immediately connected by Paul with "long-suffering," which intimates a tolerance free from the spirit of revenge. This is to be expressed in action by mutual forbearance which indicates the ability to continue to love even when conscious of faults which displease and offend. It is indeed with the word "love" that Paul closes this description of the temper in which the unity of the church is to be maintained. "Forbearing one another in love," writes the apostle, for in love forbearance is to have its motive and life. It is love that "beareth all things," "endureth all things."

The practice of such virtues and the consequent maintenance of Christian unity requires conscious effort. The church includes in its membership Jews and Gentiles, wise and ignorant, rich and poor, men and women of all races and classes. When such different dispositions, tastes, and personalities are involved, it is evident that the preservation of harmony is no slight achievement. Only by "giving diligence," by persistent effort, by fixed determination, by heroic perseverance, can "the unity of the Spirit" be kept "in the bond of peace." Thus peace must be the relation in which Christians live, if unity is to be maintained. It must be the tie which like a firm cord binds them together. It is "the bond" in which the unity is preserved.

This unity is "of the Spirit," that is, one which the Spirit produces. Whether or not it be expressed in external organization, in form of worship, in written creed, the essential unity here in mind is a unity of life, of sympathy, of interest, and of aim. It is a unity which has its source in the working of the Spirit of God. It is an existing unity. Christians are urged to guard it as something already in their possession. As such they are to "keep" it with watchful care. Just because it has been secured, because it has been produced by the Spirit, because it is a glorious fact, therefore believers are urged to manifest the virtue and to put forth the effort by which it can be maintained and made manifest.

The description of this existing unity which Paul proceeds to give is comprehensive and unique. It is sevenfold, or composed of seven elements. "There is one body, and one Spirit . . . one hope . . . one Lord, one faith, one baptism, one God and Father." These seven are often resolved into three, centering in the names of the Trinity, the "Spirit," the "Lord," the "Father." The first expresses the unity of the church itself—"one body," "one Spirit," "one hope." The second relates to the instruments of that unity—"one Lord, one faith, one baptism." The third points to the divine Author of this unity—the "one God and Father of all."

"There is one body," the universal church of Christ, the fellowship of believers, the mystical body in which all who belong to Christ are members. This is an inspiring fact. There is but one church. No matter how many outward divisions may appear to separate Christians, in spite of sects and schisms and denominations and names, "there is one body." Paul does not pray for church unity. He rejoices in it. He urges Christians to believe it, to regard it, to express it. The bounden duty of all who profess the name of Christ is to make evident in life and service the essential vital unity of the Christian church.

"There is one body, and one Spirit"—one body just because there is one Spirit. By his operation and agency men are brought into the membership of the body. As Paul wrote to the Corinthians, "In one Spirit were we all baptized into one body." As individual members are submissive to the Spirit, as they are led by the Spirit, the more eager will they be to preserve the unity and peace of the church. A Christian who is "filled with the Holy Spirit" is never factious, disagreeable, or fond of contention.

The spiritual unity of Christians is quite in accord with the blessed invitation of the gospel which they have accepted. "Even as also ye were called," writes Paul, "in one hope of your calling." This "hope" is the hope of salvation. Its nature is not that of a vague dream or expectation, but a confident assurance. Its content includes the redemption of body and spirit, a present life of service, and an immortality of glory. There is no hope like this. That it will be fully realized the Holy Spirit himself is the seal and the earnest. In this "one hope" all Christians share. Surely it should be a bond of union and its possession should incline them to maintain peace and unity with their fellow heirs, members of the same body.

The unity of the church is further emphasized by the fact that there is "one Lord," whom all Christians acknowledge and obey. The Lord Jesus Christ is, for a true believer, not only the Savior through whom his hope is to be fulfilled, but also the Lord to whose will he must submit. It is the recognition of the sole Lordship of Christ that brings believers together and enables them to recognize their oneness in him. He is the Head of his body, the church, but he is likewise the Lord and Master of each believing soul. The acknowledgment of this relationship inclines the believer to an attitude of sympathy and affection toward all who likewise serve and honor Christ.

There is "one faith," namely, the saving trust, the loving obedience, which unites believers to their Master and Lord. It is for all, the same in its essence as it is the same in its object. When such faith is real and vital it cannot fail to inspire sympathy for fellow believers and a desire for unity in the body of Christ.

So, too, there is "one baptism." Men may differ as to its mode. They may associate with it a variety of conceptions. However, its essential meaning is always the same. It is a confession of faith in Christ and a seal of membership in his body. To disturb the peace of the church or to interfere with the fellowship of believers is to break the vows of Baptism and to renounce allegiance to Christ.

Supreme and last among the elements of unity Paul mentions "one God and Father of all." The conception of "one God" is a commonplace with us; it was not so to the pagans in the days of Paul. There was in the conception something startling and revolutionary. They were familiar with "gods many, and lords many." To the Jew the unity of God was a fundamental belief. So it is to the Christian. The further conception that God is the Father of all is even more significant. As the theme under discussion is that of Christian unity, the idea here is that of the Father of all believers, the Father of the new creation, rather than that of the universal Fatherhood of God. He is "over all, and through all, and in all." This threefold relation indicates his sovereign power, his pervasive action, and his indwelling presence. Surely those who claim the privileges of "sonship" and "adoption" must seek to live in relations of harmony with their fellow members in the household of faith. Thus each element of this sevenfold unity gives an added force to the exhortation of the apostle "to keep the unity of the Spirit in the bond of peace."

This existing unity of the church is perfectly consistent, however, with the widest variety among its members and with the greatest diversity in the gifts which they severally possess. In fact, these contrasted and dissimilar gifts are all designed to promote the unity of the church and its harmonious growth toward perfection. As the apostle states, in contrasting this unity of life with the diversity of endowments, "But unto each one of us was the grace given according to the measure of the gift of Christ." This grace had been granted to every member of the body of Christ. It had been experienced by the writer and his readers. It had resulted in many different talents and abilities, but it had come from one divine source, and was intended to prepare each member for the service of the church. Each received the grace from Christ but each in the proportion which Christ was pleased to bestow. To one it was granted in larger measure, to another in smaller, but in every case it came from Christ and always with the same purpose. For every member of the church there is work to do, and for its accomplishment there is a share in the inexhaustible grace of Christ.

The fact that the ascended Christ does thus bestow upon his church gifts for service is illustrated by a quotation from the Sixty-eighth Psalm:

"When he ascended on high, he led captivity captive,
    And gave gifts unto men."

It is apparent that Paul quotes the words with considerable freedom, and introduces rather definite changes. This is evident when we compare his quotation with the lines of the psalm as they are commonly rendered:

"Thou hast ascended on high, thou hast led away captives;
 Thou hast received gifts among men."

The psalmist was referring to some historic event, the exact nature of which cannot be discovered. A triumphant king is receiving gifts from men. Paul, however, is justified in his application of the words, for the phrases of the psalm convey the two thoughts which he wishes to emphasize: first, the thought of victory; second, the bestowal of gifts. The idea of victory is expressed by both the phrases of the first line of Paul's quotation: "He ascended on high" and "He led captivity captive." The triumphal return of the victorious king is used to represent the glorious ascension of Christ. The leading away of captives pictures Christ's victory over sin and death and the grave.

There is nothing in the words of Paul or of the psalmist to indicate a release from imprisonment, or that those taken captive had previously been captive. The phrase used by Paul is intended to convey the conception of the psalm, "Thou hast led away captives." It is merely a description of the conquest of enemies. There is no reason to suppose that Paul refers to the redemption of Christians, nor to men who had been bound by sin, nor to evil spirits, nor to souls which had been imprisoned in hades. The reference means no more or less than all that is included in the triumphant ascension of Christ.

Further to emphasize this triumph, Paul pauses to dwell on the word "ascended" and to remind his readers that the glory of this victory can be measured only by the depth to which Christ descended and the glory to which he was subsequently exalted. "Now this, He ascended," writes the apostle in an impressive parenthesis, "what is it but that he also descended into the lower parts of the earth? He that descended is the same also that ascended far above all the heavens, that he might fill all things."

The descent of Christ refers to his coming down from heaven and to all that he endured in accomplishing his redeeming work. His ascension describes not merely his withdrawal from the earth into the sphere of the unseen, but it includes his being seated at the right hand of God, and his being given "all authority . . . in heaven and on earth." Some interpreters understand that the phrase, "Lower parts of the earth," is intended to define merely the earth as the scene of his atoning work, lower than his throne in the heavens. Probably it refers to the fact that Christ in his voluntary humiliation became "obedient even unto death" and for three days continued in the state of the dead.

The statement that he ascended "far above all the heavens" need not imply that Paul believed in a gradation of "heavens," even though in his day it was common to refer to the "third heaven" or the "seventh heaven." The phrase rather means that Christ is above whatever heavens there are or may be. It indicates the highest possible exaltation, and the exercise of divine sovereignty. It is a figure of speech, not designed to indicate any exact locality in space, but rather the possession of supreme power. Thus Paul adds, "That he might fill all things." This sovereign omnipresence of Christ is declared to be the very purpose and result of his ascension. Christ was exalted to the place of unlimited authority that he might fill the universe with the blessings of his beneficent rule, and might give to his church all needed grace.

This rather puzzling parenthesis is to be interpreted with caution. Particularly should one exercise restraint in attempting to base inferences on questionable interpretations. The one point the apostle intends to emphasize is the triumphant ascension of Christ. However, in the entire paragraph even the ascension is not the main thought. The bestowal of gifts by the ascended Christ—this is the great fact which Paul wishes to impress. He is insisting that unity of life is quite consistent with the wide diversity of gifts bestowed by the ascended Lord with the view to the upbuilding of his body, the church.

"He gave some to be apostles"—men specially qualified and equipped for the great work of laying broad and deep the foundations of the church; men who themselves, in a true sense, formed its foundation. An apostle in the strict meaning of the word was a witness of the resurrection, appointed directly by Christ, and possessing the power of working miracles. In a more general sense "apostles" included men like Barnabas and James, the brother of Jesus; and even today there are men of power and unusual gifts who in many lands are doing truly apostolic service for the church.

"Prophets" are next mentioned. These were itinerant teachers who, under divine inspiration, instructed the church in Christian doctrine and even on occasion predicted future events. The four daughters of Philip the evangelist are said to have "prophesied."

"Evangelists," however, seem to have done the work commonly assigned to missionaries. Philip is the only one whose work is pictured in detail. His task seems not to have been that of serving churches already established, but that of a pioneer going to regions where no churches existed. Thus today, with all propriety men who are to devote their lives to work in destitute regions and foreign fields are ordained with the title of evangelists.

"Pastors and teachers" were also mentioned as gifts of the ascended Christ. They were probably engaged as the ministers of particular congregations. It would seem that the words did not describe two classes of workers but two functions of one office. These pastor-teachers had the oversight of local churches and were engaged in giving spiritual guidance and instruction.

The men who possessed special gifts were, however, but illustrations of the more general gifts granted to each and all the members of the church. In fact, these leaders and ministers were given that all believers might by them be prepared for their work of service and to enable them to build up the church. As Paul says, they were given "for the perfecting of the saints, unto the work of ministering, unto the building up of the body of Christ." These apostles and prophets and other servants of the church were intended, therefore, to prepare and equip all the members for the service which each can render in strengthening the life of the church. Thus Paul makes it plain that each member has a task to perform. Ministers are not appointed to do the work for the members, but to prepare the members for their work, that the whole church may be built up as "the body of Christ."

The purpose of Christ in the bestowal of his gifts, and the aim of Christian service, is declared to be the securing of the unity and maturity of the church. "Till we all attain," writes Paul, "unto the . . . measure of the stature of the fulness of Christ." The persons in mind are Christians, and the unity to be attained is that of a oneness of faith in Christ and of a full knowledge of Christ. In a previous verse the apostle has insisted that Christians are already united by a common faith. There is "one faith," he asserted. All realize, however, that this faith is imperfect and the knowledge of Christ is incomplete. The perfecting of this faith, the increase of this knowledge is to be sought by every member of the church; for as long as faith is imperfect and knowledge is partial, ideal unity cannot be enjoyed.

Unity, moreover, is a condition of maturity. A divided church is an immature church. The goal toward which effort should be directed is the attainment of true spiritual manhood, or, according to the expression of Paul, "till we all attain . . . unto a fullgrown man." He uses this latter phrase instead of the phrase, "Unto fullgrown men," because he is referring to the church as a whole. Individual Christians who are factious and contentious show themselves to be in a state of spiritual infancy. So the entire church of Christ will reach maturity only as it expresses and maintains "the unity of the Spirit in the bond of peace."

This spiritual maturity is further defined as "the measure of the stature of the fulness of Christ," that is, the very standard of perfection of Christ himself. When the church, which is his body, shall be in full possession of all the graces and qualities which are in Christ, the Head, then indeed its maturity will be attained. How perfectly this can be realized in this present life or age it may be useless to argue. It is at least an ideal which there should be a ceaseless effort to approach.

This high goal has been set before the church, and spiritual leaders have been given to the church, in order "that we may be no longer children, tossed to and fro and carried about with every wind of doctrine" but may grow together, into a complete unity, as a body of which Christ is the Head. Thus spiritual infancy is manifest not only by lack of unity, but also by instability of belief. Immature Christians are easily turned from the faith. They are unstable as the waves of the sea, and tossed about restlessly by every breath of false doctrine. Thus they are in great peril, for false teachers are ever present and eager to deceive. Their methods are characterized by dishonesty and trickery. Their aim is to lead men from the truth into a false way of life.

While believers were exposed to such dangers, they had been given, on the other hand, apostles and prophets and evangelists and pastors and teachers to guard them against error. They should, therefore, be loyal to the truth and animated by love, and grow out of spiritual childhood into a mature Christian life.

It is difficult to say whether the word translated "speaking truth" should not be rendered "dealing truly," or "cherishing truth." As it is directed toward those who were in danger of being misled by false teachers, it probably indicates a loyal adherence to truth, both by way of confession and action.

To this word is added the significant phrase, "In love," for no amount of loyalty to the truth, however expressed, is a sign of spiritual maturity unless it is accompanied by sympathy and charity and love.

One might imagine that Paul had written this message for the present day. On the one hand there are many teachers of error, masquerading under Christian names, who seek to seduce men from Christian faith and life. On the other, there are those who boast their loyalty to Christian doctrine who are guilty of deception and falsehood and are exponents of malice and ill will.

Devotion to the truth and obedience to the law of love are conditions of that unity and maturity of the church which Christ has in view, and which can be secured as the members "grow up in all things into him, who is the head." As Christians are to strive to attain the likeness of Christ, so, too, they must grow into ever more complete union with him. The more complete the union, the more rapid will be the attainment. Earlier in the epistle the church has been called "the body of Christ." Here Christ is designated "the head," and Paul sets forth the relation of the members of the body to Christ and to one another. The aim of this relation is one of unity and a growth to maturity, the moral element and condition of this growth being love. This unity and growth, however, have their source in Christ. It is by vital contact with him that spiritual life is sustained and "increase" is given to the body.

As a result of this relation to Christ, the entire church is "fitly framed and knit together." Just as in the human body the different members come into contact with each other at the joints, and as each joint supplies nourishment and unites the several parts, so in the Christian church there is a place and a function for each member. Each one has a gift from Christ. Each one receives life and grace from Christ, and it is by the harmonious and helpful activity of each, in right relation to the other members, that the whole body is being upbuilt. "Through that which every joint supplieth, according to the working in due measure of each several part," writes Paul, there results "the increase of the body unto the building up of itself in love."

Thus the apostle describes the growth of the church. This growth is furthered by the loving cooperation of all its members and by their vital union with Christ. This growth will reach its consummation in a complete unity and in a final maturity which will represent the virtues and excellencies of Christ the Head.

B. EXHORTATIONS TO CHRISTIAN MORALITY
Chs. 4:17 to 5:21

1. THE OLD LIFE AND THE NEW Ch. 4:17-24

17 This I say therefore, and testify in the Lord, that ye no longer walk as the Gentiles also walk, in the vanity of their mind, 18 being darkened in their understanding, alienated from the life of God, because of the ignorance that is in them, because of the hardening of their heart; 19 who being past feeling gave themselves up to lasciviousness, to work all uncleanness with greediness. 20 But ye did not so learn Christ; 21 if so be that ye heard him, and were taught in him, even as truth is in Jesus: 22 that ye put away, as concerning your former manner of life, the old man, that waxeth corrupt after the lusts of deceit; 23 and that ye be renewed in the spirit of your mind, 24 and put on the new man, that after God hath been created in righteousness and holiness of truth.

With the opening of this fourth chapter the apostle began the practical portion of his epistle. An exhortation that his readers should live in a manner worthy of their Christian privileges passed into a more specific plea that they should seek to promote the unity of the church.

He now turns to address them as members of society, and describes the character of the life they should live, first in general (vs. 17-24) and then in the following paragraphs (chs. 4:25 to 6:9) more in detail. This general

description is both negative (vs. 17-19) and positive (vs.
20-24). The readers are warned against all conformity
to their old pagan mode of life; and then they are encouraged to live as becomes those who have a true knowledge
of Christ.

"This I say therefore," writes the apostle as he resumes
the exhortation "to walk worthily of the calling wherewith" they were called (vs. 1-3). "This I say therefore,
and testify in the Lord." These added phrases indicate the
intensity of Paul's emotion. "Testify" is a word used in
solemn protest, or in an appeal to God. Furthermore, the
injunction which follows is made "in the Lord," that is, in
the name of Christ, or by one so conscious of his fellowship and union with Christ that he speaks with divine authority; and he speaks to those who, as followers of Christ,
are expected to heed and to obey the precept of his apostle.

This, then, is the exhortation so solemnly introduced:
"That ye no longer walk as the Gentiles also walk." Here
is an implied compliment. Paul does not here compare his
readers with "other Gentiles," as some versions of this
verse declare. He indicates that his readers are no longer
to be regarded as Gentiles. They are now "fellow-citizens
with the saints, and of the household of God." However,
they are surrounded by heathen associates. They are
tempted at every turn by pagan customs. They are en-
ticed by every conceivable influence to fall back into their
former manner of living. What that manner was—or at
least what was the character of the pagan world of his own
day—Paul proceeds to declare. It is a lurid picture, con-
densed but sufficiently inclusive. The lines are exactly
those of the first chapter of his epistle to the Romans. Yet
in some respects the features, which here are quite as vivid,
bear a message even more profound. Paul describes the
mental and spiritual condition which has resulted in a state
of moral profligacy and shame.

It was a condition of aimlessness and wicked folly, for
the Gentiles were walking "in the vanity of their mind." It

was a state of spiritual ignorance and blindness for they were "darkened in their understanding." The "mind" denotes not merely the intellect, but the faculty of discerning moral and spiritual truth. The "understanding" may be regarded as the reason in action. It includes the ideas not only of thinking but of feeling and desiring. These phrases therefore describe the whole moral and spiritual character of the heathen world. With all its boasted wisdom this world was moving in a sphere of illusions and unreality. It was unable to discover truth. It was concerned with shadows and absorbed in delusions. It was striving after vanity and after things devoid of worth. Reason, which should have been its guide, was itself in darkness. The mental and moral faculties were impotent. They produced no sound theory of life, nothing rational in conduct. Everywhere futility and frivolity, blindness and perversity held their sway.

Men were "alienated from the life of God." Being estranged from him they had no share in the spiritual life which he imparts to those who trust and love him. Such a life was wholly foreign to their nature. Paul intimates that this alienation has resulted from the perversion of mind and the darkened understanding which he has just described. He now states even more definitely that it is "because of the ignorance that is in them" and "because of the hardening of their heart."

Thus it is ignorance which keeps men from God. If men knew him they would be eager to walk with him, to serve him, to worship him. Ignorance is the enemy and not the mother of devotion. The most severe indictment of the ancient world was that it "knew not God." It was an indictment because the ignorance as described by Paul was ingrained and deep-seated and culpable. It was not merely casual and superficial and excusable. It was "because of the hardening of their heart."

This latter clause explains the alienation from God, and also the ignorance which was a cause of this alienation.

These men might have known God had they sought to find him. He was revealed to them in nature and in the light of conscience. God had "left not himself without witness." However they did not recognize God in his revelation. This was not because they lacked the faculty, but because they had no desire. They thrust from them all God's messages and remained in ignorance of him because their hearts were hardened toward all the impulses that proceed from the revelation of God.

This condition of mental impotence and spiritual darkness and estrangement from God had resulted in a state of moral degradation and shameless sin. They are described as men "who being past feeling gave themselves up to lasciviousness, to work all uncleanness with greediness." They were morally insensible. Their hearts were callous and had lost all feeling for the rebukes of conscience. They had abandoned themselves to the grossest sensuality, so that they might indulge greedily in every kind of uncleanness.

Surely such a life was not consistent with Christian faith or doctrine. Such a "walk" was not worthy of the followers of the Master. Therefore, in encouraging his readers to avoid the ways of the world, Paul emphatically contrasts the knowledge and the conduct of true believers with the life and character of unconverted Gentiles. "But ye did not so learn Christ," writes the apostle. Such a life as he has described is contrary to Christ. When the gospel was preached to them they had been taught that discipleship to Christ required the renouncing of the old pagan vices and the living of a new spiritual and holy life.

"If so be that ye heard him, and were taught in him" does not imply any doubt as to the fact. The clauses rather intimate that these things can be taken for granted. The words may be rendered, "As it may be assumed that Christ was the sum and substance of the message ye received, and that after accepting him ye were instructed in vital fellowship with him."

The manner and character of this instruction is further defined as being "even as truth is in Jesus." In the historical Christ, in Jesus of Nazareth, are embodied the true standards of living, the virtues, the motives, the purity, the holiness, which his followers are expected to accept, to assume, to reproduce. The Christ of the gospel is in the fullest sense "the way, and the truth, and the life."

Therefore, as applied to those who accept him as Lord, the teaching in its substance is this, namely, that they must "put away" the vanities and vices of the pagan world, and must "put on" the virtues which belong to the new life of Christian holiness.

The content, therefore, of their Christian instruction was, described negatively, "that ye put away, as concerning your former manner of life, the old man, that waxeth corrupt after the lusts of deceit." The expression, "The old man," denotes the former self, unregenerate, and fashioned according to the life of the heathen world. This self was by its very nature in a condition of advancing corruption and ruin, in consequence of its own sinful lusts and passions. These lusts are depicted as the instruments of deceit. They are ever used to offer men the highest gratification while in reality they bring destruction.

From this negative content of Christian instruction Paul turns to describe it positively: "That ye be renewed in the spirit of your mind, and put on the new man, that after God hath been created in righteousness and holiness of truth."

Undoubtedly every Christian has been "born again," and has been the recipient of a new life principle. However, this is only the beginning of a process which must be advanced. One should seek for continual spiritual renewal and development. "The spirit" as here used by Paul denotes the high faculty by which man can enjoy fellowship with God. The "mind" is the faculty of feeling and understanding and willing. It is the instrument of the spirit. The quickened spirit furnishes pure and right impulses and motives to the mind, through which it acts.

This renewal of the spiritual faculty, or of the moral personality, is indeed the work of the Holy Spirit. However, his power is operative only in those lives which are surrendered to Christ and are seeking to "put away" the things which are contrary to his will and to show those virtues which Christ himself manifested.

Thus in addition to putting away "the old man," one is urged to "put on the new man." This new nature, this ideal humanity, which Christ has brought into being, must be appropriated in ever-increasing fullness by each of his followers. It is a new self, a new character, which accords perfectly with the will of God and this in two particulars, "in righteousness and holiness." The former expresses the right conduct of a Christian toward his fellow men; the latter his right conduct toward God. Both are expressions and results of the truth which has been proclaimed in the gospel. They should prove that they have been privileged to "learn Christ," and to be "taught in him, even as truth is in Jesus."

Thus, in contrast with the spiritual darkness and the moral impurity of the world about him, the Christian should be experiencing a continual renewal of mind and heart and should be assuming ever more completely a life and character which are after the likeness of Christ and conformed to the image and the will of God.

2. HEATHEN VICES AND CHRISTIAN VIRTUES
Chs. 4:25 to 5:2

25 Wherefore, putting away falsehood, speak ye truth each one with his neighbor: for we are members one of another. 26 Be ye angry, and sin not: let not the sun go down upon your wrath: 27 neither give place to the devil. 28 Let him that stole steal no more: but rather let him labor, working with his hands the thing that is good, that he may have whereof to give to him that hath need. 29 Let no corrupt speech proceed out of your mouth, but such as

*is good for edifying as the need may be, that it may give
grace to them that hear. 30 And grieve not the Holy Spirit
of God, in whom ye were sealed unto the day of redemption. 31 Let all bitterness, and wrath, and anger, and
clamor, and railing, be put away from you, with all malice:
32 and be ye kind one to another, tenderhearted, forgiving
each other, even as God also in Christ forgave you.*

*1 Be ye therefore imitators of God, as beloved children;
2 and walk in love, even as Christ also loved you, and gave
himself up for us, an offering and a sacrifice to God for an
odor of a sweet smell.*

Christians are being urged to "walk worthily" of their
high calling. The general exhortation has been to "put
away" the old life, the old self, "the old man," and to put
on "the new man." More specifically now certain features
of the old and the new are mentioned and placed in striking
contrast. They form a comprehensive list of heathen vices
and Christian virtues. Falsehood is contrasted with truth,
anger with forgiveness, theft with benefaction, corrupt
speech with edifying words, bitterness with love, uncleanness with purity, drunken folly with spiritual fervor.

It is not surprising that Christians in the first century,
just emerging from paganism and surrounded by degrading customs, should need such warnings and admonitions.
It is humiliating, however, to admit that believers of the
present day, with all their advantages of inheritance and
culture, need similar exhortations. Unhappily these precepts of the apostle are not out of date.

The vices condemned and the virtues inculcated were
familiar and even commonplace in that early day as in this.
What is distinctive in Paul's teaching, however, as compared with that of moralists of the past or present, is the
ground on which his exhortations are based and the high
motives to which he appeals. He traces all moral fault to
alienation from God; he relates all virtues to faith in Christ.

The first division in this series of moral contrasts begins
with the vice of deceit and the virtue of truthfulness.

"Wherefore, putting away falsehood, speak ye truth each one with his neighbor." The "wherefore" refers back to what has just been said about the teachings of Christ. These definitely enjoined the putting away of the old vices and the putting on of "the new man." On this account, therefore, the disciple of Christ must put away falsehood and must speak the truth. The two verbs are of different tenses. The "putting away" is to be once for all; the speaking of truth is to be continuous.

"Falsehood" denotes not only lying but every form of deception. So, too, "truth" is to be spoken by each one to "his neighbor," by which term Christ taught his disciples to include all men. The special reference here, however, is to fellow Christians, as the ground given for the exhortation is this: "For we are members one of another." It is true that the human race forms a body in which we all are members. Yet the body here in mind is the church of Christ. Paul, in this epistle, is particularly concerned with unity. Nothing so divides and separates Christians as falsehood, misrepresentations, suspicion, and unscrupulous partisanship. Mutual confidence is the essential bond of Christian fellowship. It is not strange that Paul, who in exhorting the church to maintain "the unity of the Spirit in the bond of peace" insisted upon "speaking truth in love," gives as his first specific exhortation for the conduct of individual lives the putting away of falsehood and the speaking of truth.

The exhortation, "Speak ye truth each one with his neighbor," echoes an Old Testament command (Zech. 8:16). So the second exhortation, "Be ye angry, and sin not," seems to be a quotation from the Fourth Psalm (v. 4), in the form which appears in the margin of the Revised Version.

Some readers are troubled by the command, "Be ye angry," and try to soften the words to mean, "If you are angry, do not let your anger drive you to some worse sin." However, anger is not sin. It was felt and expressed by our Lord himself. There is such a thing as righteous resentment. Wrath has its proper place if directed not against the sinner but against the sin. An age may become so accustomed to injustice and impurity that the very genius for indignation is lost.

However, comparatively little indignation is righteous. Wrath is usually wrong and sinful. Resentment is commonly a feeling of wounded pride. The words of the apostle are not to be taken as an excuse for irritation and bad temper, nor to be used as a cloak for passion, malice, or revenge.

Anger is a very dangerous state of mind, particularly for weak and fallible and imperfect men. In most cases it becomes an occasion for sin. It is not to be supposed that Paul's main purpose is to encourage anger. The emphasis is to be laid upon the second part of his command, which is to be kept in mind whenever the feeling of resentment arises: "Sin not." Furthermore, Paul immediately adds, "Let not the sun go down upon your wrath." The word for "wrath" is somewhat different from the word "angry," and denotes sudden and violent exasperation. Evidently, the apostle is passing from the thought of mere innocent indignation against evil to the more common emotion of animosity or passion. In any case resentment is not to be cherished. Wrath is not to be nursed. Even righteous anger is to be controlled. It is not to be prolonged beyond the sunset, a figurative expression which well may be applied with a considerable degree of literalness. "Neither give place to the devil," writes Paul, for if anger is permitted to continue, it will give the adversary room to act, an opportunity of leading us into outbursts of passion, since angry feelings so easily result in hatred and malice and sinful words and deeds.

As Paul turns from anger to theft, he uses a very strong expression: "Let him that stole steal no more"; literally, "Let him who is stealing steal no more." The language may even imply that the old pagan vice was still practiced

by some connected with the Christian church. This is
quite credible. The new converts found it difficult to secure employment and may in certain instances have re-
lapsed into this as into other former sins. At least the
words refer to a practice which was prevalent among pagans, and in Christian assemblies there were undoubtedly
thieves who by the power of the gospel had been transformed into honest men. It may be added that even today
professing Christians have been found guilty of breaking
the commandment which this injunction embodies, namely,
"Thou shalt not steal." For stealing has other forms than
theft and robbery. It may be involved in the misuse of
trust funds, in gambling, in unfair wages, in unpaid debts,
and in other practices which the conscience of the time
may not condemn.

The virtue which Paul opposes to stealing is serving.
Not only does he insist upon honest toil, but he urges one
to labor so diligently that he may have some surplus with
which to relieve his brother who is in want. "Let him labor, working with his hands the thing that is good," writes
the apostle, "that he may have whereof to give to him that
hath need." Theft in all its forms misappropriates to one's
own use the results of labor which belong to another.
Thus, by way of contrast, the highest motive for patient
and humble toil is the desire thereby to acquire the power
to relieve those who are in distress. The supreme inspiration in labor is not personal gain but sympathetic service.
When a truly Christian spirit pervades the sphere of industry, the most pressing economic problems will be solved.

Service to others can be rendered, however, not only by
deeds but by words. Sometimes a message of cheer has
more value than a gift of gold. Therefore Paul warns his
readers against allowing any bad or worthless utterance to
escape their lips, and urges the use of such words as will
strengthen and help. "Let no corrupt speech proceed out
of your mouth" is the injunction. The reference probably
is not specifically to impure and foul language. This is

mentioned a few verses farther on in this epistle. "Corrupt" must include here what it means in such phrases as a "corrupt tree," or "corrupt fruit." It denotes that which is worthless, profitless, inane, inept, of no use to anyone.

Such unwholesome, idle, useless talk is all too prevalent among Christians of the present age. With it Paul contrasts "such as is good for edifying as the need may be." The phrase seems to describe such speech as will be helpful to others according to the need of the occasion. Speech of this kind "may give grace to them that hear." It not only may be gracious but it may be an actual means of grace to the hearers. It may impart to them a blessing and a spiritual benefit.

On the contrary "corrupt speech" not only may injure one's fellowmen but also may be an offense against "the Holy Spirit of God, in whom ye were sealed unto the day of redemption." The very warning implies a blessed reality. It assumes that the Holy Spirit is an abiding presence, a comforter, by whom every Christian is indwelt. Yet because of his nearness one must avoid those sins of the tongue which are certain to give him offense.

To make the warning more solemn, the comforter is called "the Holy Spirit," and as holiness is the very essence of his being, unholy speech must be repugnant to him. He is also called the "Spirit of God," and as love is the supreme attribute of God, it is evident that God must be displeased with all forms of speech which may cause injury to others.

Still further is the injunction strengthened by the reminder that the Holy Spirit is the Person in fellowship with whom and by whose influence every believer is "sealed unto the day of redemption." A seal is a mark of ownership and of security. It may be a stamp of likeness. Christians belong to God. They are being transformed into his image. They are being kept by his power until the day when Christ is to appear, when redemption will be complete, when "we shall be like him." How careful,

therefore, should Christians be not to offend him by whom
we are being guarded, not to grieve him to whom we belong, not to act contrary to the nature of him into whose
likeness we are being changed.   It is by such solemn considerations that we are warned against all forms of corrupt
speech.

The same considerations, however, should keep us from
all unkind dispositions and deeds.   So, last of all in this
series of Christian virtues and pagan vices, Paul contrasts
bitterness of spirit with love.   "Let all bitterness, and
wrath, and anger, and clamor, and railing, be put away
from you, with all malice."   "Bitterness" describes the
resentful, harsh, implacable temper, which in all its forms
must be put away.   With wrath and anger the apostle had
dealt already.   (Ch. 4:26.)   As here forbidden, "wrath"
denotes fury, or the temporary outburst of passion, and
"anger" the settled dispostion of indignation and anger.
Both have their root in the bitter and resentful spirit mentioned previously.   "Clamor" and "railing" are the audi-
ble expressions of the tempers just described.   Clamor is
the loud outburst of an angry man; railing is his slanderous,
insulting, and abusive speech.   All these feelings and expressions are to be "put away," together with "all malice,"
or every kind of ill will, malignity, and spite.

By way of contrast Paul urges the supreme Christian
motive of love.   "Be ye kind one to another, tenderhearted, forgiving each other."   Kindness is gentleness
toward evildoers; to be tenderhearted is to feel toward
them warm sympathy and love.   Both these sentiments
find their specific expression in forgiveness.   Forgiveness,
again, finds its model and impelling motive in the forgiveness of God, "even as God also in Christ forgave you."
This rendering of the last clause is far better than the familiar translation, "As God for Christ's sake hath forgiven
you."   The God who "forgave" was the God who was himself manifest in the suffering, atoning Christ.   The forgiveness was "in Christ."   The expression is parallel to those

words of the apostle, "God was in Christ reconciling the world unto himself, not reckoning unto them their trespasses."

It is such sublime realities that Paul appeals to in enforcing his exhortation to kindness and tenderness and to a forgiving spirit. Thus the atoning work of Christ is not only a great doctrine of our faith; it is also an example in life and a motive to forgiving love.

The beginning here of a new chapter is rather unfortunate, for the first two verses of chapter five continue to dwell on the supreme example of divine forgiveness. "Be ye therefore imitators of God," writes Paul, referring by the "therefore" to kindness and forgiveness as the specific sphere in which the example of God is to be followed. The imitation is urged not only on the ground of benefits received, but because believers are in a unique sense "children of God" and particularly are his "beloved children." The reasoning is like that of the "disciple whom Jesus loved" as he writes, "If God so loved us, we also ought to love one another." Even more fully does the argument follow the words of the Master when he bids his followers imitate the forgiveness and compassion of their Father who "maketh his sun to rise on the evil and the good, and sendeth rain on the just and the unjust." This exhortation to follow the example of God is concluded by Christ in these words: "Ye therefore shall be perfect, as your heavenly Father is perfect."

The climax of the paragraph is reached as Paul adds, "And walk in love." The "walk" of a Christian indicates throughout this epistle the whole course and conduct of life and particularly its habitual acts and pursuits. The command is in effect, "Live and act lovingly." The imitation of God is therefore to be manifest in the practical and continual deeds of daily activity. The motive and pattern for such a walk as here specified is the self-sacrificing love of Christ: "Even as Christ also loved you, and gave himself up for us, an offering and a sacrifice to God for an odor of a sweet smell."

Thus the love of the Father and the love of the Son are mentioned in parallel terms. The one is the love of pity and of pardon; the other, the love of service and sacrifice which reached its culmination in the cross. It is hardly necessary to note that the death of Christ was not designed to secure for men the love of God. It was God himself who was acting and manifesting himself in the atoning, suffering Christ. It was the Son who submitted himself in love, even enduring death in unswerving loyalty to the Father's will. This complete submission and obedience were well pleasing to the Father, so that the death of Christ for us can be described in terms of the Old Testament ritual as a sacrifice "for an odor of a sweet smell." It thus indicates an offering "acceptable, well pleasing to God."

Love, then, is to be the rule of the Christian life. It is to be a love which puts aside all bitterness and malice, a love which forgives and forgets. Yet it is also to be no weak sentiment which tolerates wrong or confines itself to empty words of sympathy. It must be an emotion which is regulated by the holy will of God and expressed in deeds of self-sacrificing service worthy of those who have taken up the cross and are following him who "gave himself up for us."

3. DARKNESS AND LIGHT   Ch. 5:3-14

3 But fornication, and all uncleanness, or covetousness, let it not even be named among you, as becometh saints; 4 nor filthiness, nor foolish talking, or jesting, which are not befitting: but rather giving of thanks. 5 For this ye know of a surety, that no fornicator, nor unclean person, nor covetous man, who is an idolater, hath any inheritance in the kingdom of Christ and God. 6 Let no man deceive you with empty words: for because of these things cometh the wrath of God upon the sons of disobedience. 7 Be not ye therefore partakers with them; 8 for ye were once darkness, but are now light in the Lord: walk as children of light 9 (for the fruit of the light is in all goodness and righteousness and truth), 10 proving what is well-pleasing unto the

*Lord; 11 and have no fellowship with the unfruitful works
of darkness, but rather even reprove them; 12 for the
things which are done by them in secret it is a shame even
to speak of. 13 But all things when they are reproved are
made manifest by the light: for everything that is made
manifest is light. 14 Wherefore he saith, Awake, thou
that sleepest, and arise from the dead, and Christ shall
shine upon thee.*

Sins of ill will were no more prevalent in the pagan
world than were sins of impurity. Therefore, when the
apostle has warned Christian converts against yielding to
anger and hatred, he turns to remind them of the more
severe temptations of degrading and corrupt forms of love.
He contrasts the prevalent vices of the society by which
they were surrounded with the stainless virtues of a Christian life. To emphasize this contrast he employs the
figures of "light" and "darkness" and centers his exhortation in the comprehensive command, "Walk as children of
light."

The moral darkness which surrounded these Christians
was indeed appalling. The "fornication" and "uncleanness" which Paul severely prohibits were commonly regarded as matters of indifference. They were practiced
and countenanced in all circles without scruple and without shame. Closely associated with this prevalent immorality was the other enslaving vice of the heathen world,
namely, "covetousness." These vices, Paul declares, are
not even to be named among Christians, much less to be
practiced by them. The reason is obvious. Christians are
to live "as becometh saints." As such they belong to God.
They have been separated unto his service. They must,
therefore, keep themselves free from practices which the
laws of God forbid, however well these practices accord
with the customs of the times.

Nor would it be congruous for them to be guilty of
"filthiness" in act or word, or "foolish talking, or jesting."
The apostle must not be understood to condemn hu-

mor. A sense of humor is a precious gift. Even in the church most serious troubles are caused by men who lack this saving grace. They take themselves too seriously, and clothe all prospects with a somber hue. They fail to see how absurd they make themselves and what grotesque situations they create. Wit and cleverness and a keen sense of the ridiculous are the salt which savors friendly intercourse and the cheer which makes tolerable many of life's distresses.

The rebuke was intended rather for the low frivolity which makes light of sin, and the scurrilous talk which disgraces human speech and cannot possibly be tolerated in a follower of Christ. As Paul mildly states, such conversation is "not befitting." Instead of these expressions of an impure mind, the thoughts of a Christian should be filled with love and gratitude to God which flow forth in "giving of thanks," in words of gratitude and praise.

Paul insists that he is telling his readers nothing new, as he continues to forbid any complicity with the prevailing sins of the age. "For this ye know of a surety, that no fornicator, nor unclean person, nor covetous man, who is an idolater, hath any inheritance in the kingdom of Christ and God." It is noticeable that here again covetousness is put upon a level with gross sins of the flesh. Greed is described as idolatry, for it is the debasing worship of gold. Surely no Christian could suppose that one guilty of such faults can belong to that Kingdom which is in its essence love and joy and peace, and which is yet to find its consummation in the perfected and heavenly reign of Christ.

However, there are always those who find excuses for sin. They are saying today that strict morality is puritanical, and is the mere relic of outgrown standards of life. "Let no man deceive you with empty words," writes the apostle. All specious arguments, all false reasoning to the contrary, the fact is that "because of these things cometh the wrath of God upon the sons of disobedience."

"The wrath of God" denotes his displeasure with sin, which cannot fail to be expressed in the loss and suffering and pain in which wrongdoing results both here and hereafter. This must inevitably rest upon those who willfully defy the laws of God and reject his offers of mercy and grace and love.

In the vices practiced by these "sons of disobedience," Christians are to have no part. "Be not ye therefore partakers with them," writes the apostle. The reason for such a prohibtion is this: "For ye were once darkness, but are now light in the Lord." The state and condition when such sins were possible and natural have, for believers, long since passed. They "were once darkness." So ignorant were they of God and his will, so absolutely identified with evil, that they were not only in the dark; they were darkness itself. Such they had been. Now, however, in striking contrast, they were "light." The truth of the gospel had so penetrated their souls and transfigured their lives that they were not only morally and spiritually illumined; they were not only walking in the light; they were themselves "light." They were wholly possessed by the truth, and were centers which radiated the truth. This was because of their relationship to Christ who is the "light of the world." By fellowship with him they had been transformed. They are now "light in the Lord."

In view of such a moral transformation comes the command, "Walk as children of light." That command is of deep significance. It indicates, first of all, that Christians do differ from the men and women of the world. There is a reality in conversion, in the "new birth," in being "born of the Spirit." In the second place it indicates that the instrument which effects this transformation is truth. Creed does determine character. Belief does affect conduct. Faith does manifest itself in life. In the third place the command intimates that even Christians are tempted to fall back into former ways of living, and need to be exhorted to "walk" continually and consistently as becomes those who belong to the realm of "light" and whose very nature is "light."

The essential features of such a walk are declared to be "goodness and righteousness and truth." The first of these denotes kindness, or beneficence, or goodness in action. The second indicates uprightness or moral rectitude. The third is the opposite of falsehood or hypocrisy and signifies honesty and sincerity. The three great essentials of Christian morality are thus set forth in terms of the good, the just, and the true. These are all pictured as the moral results of accepting the gospel light: "For the fruit of the light is in all goodness and righteousness and truth."

This last clause is in a parenthesis. However, it is inseparable from the command to "walk as children of light." It explains and enforces that command. It indicates that conduct of any other kind would be improper and incongruous for those who have been transfigured by the knowledge of Christ and through fellowship with him.

The command is further enforced by the phrase, "Proving what is well-pleasing unto the Lord." "Proving" here means "finding out by experiment and experience." This is an infallible rule of a true Christian life. It must correspond to "the good and acceptable and perfect will of God."

"Have no fellowship with the unfruitful works of darkness," continues the apostle, "but rather even reprove them." He is further forbidding Christian converts from having any part in the impure practices of the pagan world by which they were surrounded. These practices are termed "unfruitful." They yield no profit, no reward. However, they are not lacking in results. They produce bitterness and disgrace and pain. They do not yield "the fruit of the light," "goodness and righteousness and truth."

These practices Christians must "even reprove." It is not enough for them silently to abstain. They must rebuke them, not only by their own pure lives and consistent moral conduct, but by open censure, designed to show the

evil and peril of such practices and to lead to their condemnation and abandonment. How necessary it was to
expose and restrain such vices is emphasized by the words
which follow: "For the things which are done by them in
secret it is a shame even to speak of." Not all pagan
vices were of this unspeakable character. Some were—
particularly those that were practiced "in secret." Such
needed severe rebuke.

As to the exact method of such public reproof, great care
should be exercised at all times. Christians are not called
upon to act continually as moral detectives and to spy out
the secret sins of their fellowmen. Nor does the rebuke of
evil need to include the publication of all the loathsome
details of crime. Some evils are not checked but aggra-
vated by publicity. Some forms of sin are actually unspeakable. Nevertheless "children of light" should not
seem to connive at evil, but must discover proper ways of
rebuking immorality and vice.

They are encouraged to such a course by the assurance
that such vices, when rightly rebuked, are revealed in their
odious character by the light of Christian truth, and may
even be displaced, when so revealed, by the virtues of the
Christian life. Such seems to be the general import of the
rather obscure clauses, "But all things when they are reproved are made manifest by the light: for everything that
is made manifest is light." Not always does reproof have
such happy results. Normally, however, the consequence
of moral illumination is moral transformation. In this
sense it is true that "anything that is illuminated turns into
light." This becomes most evident when it is remembered that Christians are to employ the "light" of the gospel when they "reprove" the evils of the world. When
the proclamation of this truth is the instrument with which
they work, it is easy to see how, without offense, the most
unspeakable vices can be rebuked, and how the most
grievous offenders can become "children of light."

That such blessed results may be attained by a faithful

manifestation of the light, Paul encourages his readers to
believe, as he quotes what may possibly be the fragment
of an ancient hymn: "Awake, thou that sleepest, and arise
from the dead, and Christ shall shine upon thee." There
is here a certain verbal resemblance to the words of Isa.
60:1: "Arise, shine; for thy light is come, and the glory of
Jehovah is risen upon thee." If this was in the mind of the
apostle, he evidently used great liberty with the quotation.
The meaning of his words, however, is clear. The condition of the "sons of disobedience," whose vices darkened
the face of the pagan world, was that of moral slumber—
indeed, that of moral and spiritual death. The proclamation of the gospel, while rebuking their vices, is a call to
new life. If they will rouse themselves from their moral
stupor and turn from their practices of shame, the glorious
light which streams from the face of Christ will shine upon
them, their souls will be illumined, they themselves will become "children of light."

4. PAGAN FOLLY AND CHRISTIAN FERVOR
Ch. 5:15-21

*15 Look therefore carefully how ye walk, not as unwise,
but as wise; 16 redeeming the time, because the days are
evil. 17 Wherefore be ye not foolish, but understand what
the will of the Lord is. 18 And be not drunken with wine,
wherein is riot, but be filled with the Spirit; 19 speaking
one to another in psalms and hymns and spiritual songs,
singing and making melody with your heart to the Lord;
20 giving thanks always for all things in the name of our
Lord Jesus Christ to God, even the Father; 21 subjecting
yourselves one to another in the fear of Christ.*

In his series of pagan vices and Christian virtues, the last
contrast drawn by the apostle is between the reckless folly
of the pagan world and the spiritual fervor which should
characterize the followers of Christ. "Look therefore carefully how ye walk, not as unwise, but as wise," is the in-

junction of the apostle. Thus for the fifth time in this practical portion of his epistle does he use the term "walk" to describe the conduct, the habit of life, becoming to Christians. First of all, as members of the church, Christians are "to walk worthily" of their calling by giving "diligence to keep the unity of the Spirit in the bond of peace." Then, as members of society, they are to "no longer walk as the Gentiles also walk, in the vanity of their mind." Furthermore, they are to "walk in love." In the fourth place, they are to "walk as children of light." Here they are enjoined to "walk, not as unwise, but as wise." Each of these phrases characterizes Christian conduct as set forth in the paragraph in which it is found. Thus together they form at once a division and a summary of these first five paragraphs in which the great doctrines of the epistle are applied to daily life.

The fourth exhortation to "walk as children of light" is here resumed: "Look therefore carefully how ye walk." The command, however, is made more specific by the phrase, "Not as unwise, but as wise." Christians, particularly in their social life, are to avoid the frivolity, the thoughtlessness, the folly of the age, and are to live as wise men. This wisdom should be manifest specifically in "redeeming the time." This does not mean "in making the times better," nor in "making the best use of time." The word for "time" more strictly denotes "opportunity," or "fit time." Nor does the word "redeeming" necessitate the statement of any particular price paid. The entire phrase seems to mean "making the most of every opportunity." The wisdom of their walk would thus consist in their careful endeavor to seize upon every fitting season for doing good, and to make their own every possible occasion for the fulfillment of duty. This would indeed require promptness and discerning zeal, and a careful effort to let no opportunity pass unused.

The reason why such care should be exercised in "redeeming the time" is stated as being "because the days are evil." This does not mean merely that the times are full of trouble and difficulty, but rather that they are morally corrupt. The obstacles in the way of Christian service are therefore great, and the opportunities of turning men to light are few, so there is an evident necessity for seizing upon every occasion which may appear.

The walk of the Christian in such times needs to be characterized by true wisdom. Converts from paganism must not allow themselves to slip back into senseless folly. They dare not close their eyes to the difference between right and wrong. They must have a clear discernment of their Master's will. "Wherefore be ye not foolish," Paul insists, "but understand what the will of the Lord is." Christ is not only a sacrifice for sin; he is not only an example to be followed; he is Lord of the life. His servants must be eager to know and ready to obey his holy will. In contrast with the insensate men of the world they must have spiritual enlightenment and moral intelligence. Their lives are given dignity by the knowledge of a divine plan, and their characters are ennobled by obedience to a divine purpose.

One particular form of pagan folly is singled out for rebuke by the apostle, namely, intoxication. "And be not drunken with wine, wherein is riot," he writes. Surely no man is so senseless as the inebriate. There is no madness like that of strong drink. Intemperance results in "riot," or, as the word may mean, in dissoluteness, in debauchery, in every form of excess.

In contrast with the sinful excitements of such stimulants, and the intoxication which results from wine, the Christian is urged to be "filled with the Spirit." This phrase is quite common in the earlier chapters of The Acts. It seems to describe a state in which one is under the control of the Spirit of Christ and impelled and empowered to do his will. It was not a mystical—nor was it regarded as an exceptional—experience. It was not the prerogative of any one believer or of any one class of Christians. It was an experience frequently repeated in the life of individuals and of the church. To be "filled with the Spirit" is indeed the normal state of every follower of Christ. The supreme condition is surrender to Christ, the knowing and doing "what the will of the Lord is." It is a state which can be developed and sustained by prayer, by appropriating revealed truth, by fellowship with believers, by using the means of grace.

There is, however, one expression and consequence of being "filled with the Spirit" on which Paul here lays stress. In contrast with the ribald songs which come from the lips of one who is "drunken with wine," the Spirit-filled man will be heard singing praises to his Lord. "Speaking one to another in psalms and hymns and spiritual songs," writes Paul. It is difficult to discover the exact distinction between the three forms of praise here named. "Psalms" may refer specifically to selections from the Old Testament psalter, but many readers believe that, like "hymns" and "songs," they were compositions by members of the early church, produced under the inspiration of the Holy Spirit. Nor does it seem certain that Paul here refers to public worship. These Christians, filled with the Spirit, are to express themselves in ther social fellowship not in mere conventional forms of conversation, but by "speaking one to another" in the very language of devotion and praise.

Paul adds that their spiritual fervor is also to be expressed by "singing and making melody with your heart to the Lord." The silent music of the rejoicing heart is to accompany the praise of anointed lips. This music of the soul cannot be heard by men. It cannot be directed to men, or intended for their hearing, as much vocal music is. It is for the Lord. It is directed to him, and will be pleasing to him if inspired by his Spirit.

Materials for such songs are never lacking, for, if "filled with the Spirit," Christians will be found to be "giving thanks always for all things in the name of our Lord Jesus

Christ." The phrase "all things," as here used, does not necessarily imply hardships and sorrows and distresses. Probably in all these we should still be thankful. Paul, however, in this letter is dealing rather with the mercy and grace of God, and "the unsearchable riches of Christ." Surely, for limitless blessings continually bestowed, Christians should ever be giving thanks to God, who here, as so frequently, is called "the Father." To him we address our expressions of gratitude, when filled with his Spirit. Yet our praises are acceptable, and should ever be spoken "in the name of" his Son, "our Lord Jesus Christ." A "name" is that by which one is known. "In the name of our Lord Jesus Christ" means, therefore, "in virtue of all that Christ is known to be." He is our Lord and Master. Therefore, our praise is that of his followers. He is the divine Son, and through faith in him our thanksgiving is that of children of God. The praise which is well pleasing to the Father is Christian praise.

A fourth clause is added to indicate how Christians may express the experience of being "filled with the Spirit." It is a phrase too often neglected in this connection. It names a test of spirituality which Christians too seldom apply: "Subjecting yourselves one to another in the fear of Christ." Many persons feel that shouts of hallelujah and exulting songs and the utterance of praise in more or less "unknown tongues" are all proofs of being "filled with the Spirit." These all may be spurious and deceitful and without meaning. Submission to our fellow Christians, modesty of demeanor, humility, an unwillingness to dispute, forbearance, gentleness—these are the unmistakable proofs of the Spirit's power; for "the fruit of the Spirit is love, joy, peace, longsuffering, kindness, goodness, faithfulness, meekness, self-control." Such mutual submission to their fellow Christians should be rendered "in the fear of Christ," that is, in reverence to him who is recognized as the Lord and Master of all.

C. EXHORTATIONS TO THE CHRISTIAN FAMILY   Chs. 5:22 to 6:9

1. WIVES AND HUSBANDS   Ch. 5:22-33

22 Wives, be in subjection *unto your own husbands, as unto the Lord.   23 For the husband is the head of the wife, as Christ also is the head of the church,* being *himself the saviour of the body.   24 But as the church is subject to Christ, so* let *the wives also be to their husbands in everything.   25 Husbands, love your wives, even as Christ also loved the church, and gave himself up for it;   26 that he might sanctify it, having cleansed it by the washing of water with the word,   27 that he might present the church to himself a glorious church, not having spot or wrinkle or any such thing; but that it should be holy and without blemish. 28 Even so ought husbands also to love their own wives as their own bodies.   He that loveth his own wife loveth himself: 29 for no man ever hated his own flesh; but nourisheth and cherisheth it, even as Christ also the church;   30 because we are members of his body.   31 For this cause shall a man leave his father and mother, and shall cleave to his wife; and the two shall become one flesh.   32 This mystery is great: but I speak in regard of Christ and of the church.   33 Nevertheless do ye also severally love each one his own wife even as himself; and* let *the wife* see *that she fear her husband.*

The Epistle of Paul to the Ephesians is rightly regarded as the most profound of his writings; yet nowhere is the apostle more practical in his purpose and message.   He traces back the will of God to past eternities; he regards the church as already seated in the "heavenlies" and there revealing to "the principalities and the powers" "the manifold wisdom of God"; but he employs the main portion of his epistle with the plainest exhortations for daily life.   It is true, however, that he enforces the simplest duties by reference to the most sublime motives.   The divine mysteries with which the earlier part of the epistle is filled form the basis on which the practical precepts rest.   In fact, the latter cannot be understood unless the former are kept in mind.

Thus the instructions which Paul gives to members of the Christian family cannot be rightly interpreted unless it is kept in mind that Paul regards these members of the family as at the same time members of the church, the mystical body of Christ.   In the light of this dual relationship the commands of the apostle must be read.

His practical exhortations dealt first of all with life in the church; there the duty emphasized was "unity."   The next exhortations related to life in society; there the supreme demand was for purity.   He now deals with the Christian home, and the comprehensive word is love.

This paragraph relating to domestic life is linked to the preceding by the term "subjection."   Indeed the connection is so close that, in the original Greek, the word is not repeated but is taken for granted.   Paul has just insisted upon the mutual subjection which all Christians should show to one another.   He begins his instruction to the family by specifying the affectionate deference which married women should show to their husbands, expecting in return self-sacrificing devotion and love: "Wives, be in subjection unto your own husbands."

It is this admonition to wives which has made Paul the object of most bitter attack.   The apostle has been declared to be the enemy of women.   His teachings have been attributed to an age of darkness when women were degraded and debased by men.   On the other hand, more careful study will show that Paul has been their great emancipator.   He is the one who has insisted upon their spiritual equality with men.   Wherever his teachings have been accepted women have been enfranchised, ennobled, and given their just and proper rights.

Paul insisted upon the sanctity of family life.   He regarded the family, and not the individual, as the unit of society.   The individualist and the socialist are the sworn enemies of the family.   The former considers marriage as a contract between two parties, to be ended at any time by mutual agreement. The latter regards the state as supreme in its authority over all individuals, and as the rightful custodian of all children; the socialist is determined to destroy both the family and the church. Paul treats marriage as an inseparable union between a husband and wife, so sacred, so blessed, as to be a fit symbol of the relation between Christ and his church; and he views the family as the sphere in which the sacred rights of womanhood can best be protected and without which they cannot possibly be maintained.

It is for this reason that he insists upon those mutual relations between wives and husbands by which unity and happiness and security can be ensured to the Christian home.

The "subjection" of the wife to the husband is merely that voluntary submission of one Christian to another which regards the family as a divine institution wherein the husband has the responsibility of leadership, of support, of protection, and of loving care. This seems to be the meaning of Paul when he says, "Wives, be in subjection unto your own husbands, as unto the Lord." This subjection is therefore that of a Christian who in rendering obedience to her husband regards this obedience as rendered unto Christ; it is for his sake, and according to his will. The reason for such submission "as unto the Lord" is given in the following verse: "For the husband is the head of the wife, as Christ also is the head of the church." This Headship is because of a vital and blessed union. It is due to the relation sustained by the husband to Christ, and is like the relation of Christ to his church. It is, therefore, absolutely remote from all that is harsh or tyrannical or selfish on the part of the husband, for it is in virtue of a submission, on the part of the wife, which is that of trust and affection and devotion, like that of the church toward Christ.

The relation of Christ to the church, however, is not

only that of Head but also that of Savior: "Being himself
the saviour of the body." This, in the fullest sense, the
husband cannot be to the wife. The intimation may possibly be, however, that he is to be as far as possible her
protector and deliverer, in virtue of which the wife renders
him free and loyal allegiance.

Nevertheless, while the husband cannot be to the wife
all that Christ is to his church, the wife is to recognize the
leadership and authority of the husband in the Christian
home: "But as the church is subject to Christ, so let the
wives also be to their husbands in everything."

This subjection of a Christian wife to her husband, therefore, is evidently not that of compulsion and slavish fear
but that which comes from freedom and by which true
freedom is maintained. Furthermore, it exists, and can be
expected to endure, only where a husband manifests Christ-
like devotion and love.

It is this condition and requirement which Paul emphasizes as he now turns to set forth the duties and obligations
of husbands toward their wives. These are shown to demand a self-surrender so complete that it can be compared
with the redeeming grace of Christ: "Husbands, love your
wives, even as Christ also loved the church, and gave himself up for it." Only as one fulfills this condition of unself-
ish and sacrificial service, only when one exhibits perfect
sympathy and chivalrous care, has he the right to claim
leadership or headship in a Christian family. Paul has
nothing to say here of the rights of husbands; much less
does he countenance in the least the conduct of a man
who, by thoughtlessness or caprice, by callousness or cruelty, becomes the oppressor of a wife instead of showing
himself to be her protector and her delight.

The love of Christ, which every husband must imitate,
was manifest in that he gave himself up to die for the
church. The purpose was twofold. The first is accomplished in the present time; the second is consummated at
his return. He "gave himself up for it; that he might sanc-

tify it, having cleansed it by the washing of water with the word." Thus, as is usual in the New Testament, the death of Christ is said to effect not only a legal relation but particularly a moral charge. Christ made it possible, by his death, to secure the church for himself, to sanctify it, to set it apart for his service, and to cleanse it from all the guilt and stain of sin.

This cleansing is said to be "by the washing of water with the word." That this is a specific reference to Christian baptism is almost universally believed. However, it is quite probable that the "word" refers not merely to the confession of faith in Christ, but also to the gospel message. So that the cleansing is effected by the power of the "word," of which the water of baptism is the symbol. It is only as the Holy Spirit applies to the soul of the believer the truth of Christ's redemption that the saving work of Christ is accomplished.

This salvation, however, will not be complete until Christ reappears. Thus Paul sets forth the further purpose of the self-sacrifice of Christ, namely, "that he might present the church to himself a glorious church, not having spot or wrinkle or any such thing; but that it should be holy and without blemish." The "marriage supper of the Lamb" is still future. It is intended to represent that fuller fellowship with Christ which believers will enjoy when he returns. Then the moral perfecting which now has been begun will be complete.

The love which, for the accomplishment of such ends, impelled Christ to give himself up for the church is the example of the supreme affection to be felt by husbands toward their wives. It was the love of Christ toward his own mystical body, the church. "Even so ought husbands also to love their own wives as their own bodies." This seems to mean, not merely that husbands should love their wives as truly as they love their bodies, but rather that they should love their wives as if they were their own bodies, or as being parts of their very selves. It is thus that

Christ loves his own body, the church. So Paul continues, "He that loveth his own wife loveth himself." This is perfectly natural, if she is regarded as part of himself: "For no man ever hated his own flesh; but nourisheth and cherisheth it, even as Christ also the church." Thus, not only the sense of duty, but the instincts of nature should incline the husband, not to neglect and unkindness, but to devoted care, protection, and support. Christ so cares for his church, and for the same reason, namely, the unity which exists in both cases—the oneness of husband and wife, the oneness of Christ and his church. "Because," writes the apostle, "we are members of his body."

Further to enforce the loving conduct which a husband should show toward his wife, and to emphasize the fact of the unity which results from marriage, Paul quotes the primeval law (Gen. 2:24), in which the identity or unity of husband and wife is set forth: "For this cause," that is, in order to realize the high ideal of conjugal union, "shall a man leave his father and mother, and shall cleave to his wife; and the two shall become one flesh." Thus the narrative of the Creation, recording the divine ordinance of marriage, declares the absolute unity and identity of husband and wife. Paul adds that he finds in this ordinance of God an illustration of the union of Christ with his church. This union is a heavenly archetype of marriage, which is the highest and most sacred of all earthly relationships. Just because Christians do sustain such a union with Christ, just because they are members of his body, the Christian husband should be the more unfailing in his devotion toward his wife.

That marriage is a type of Christ's relation to his church is a truth of profound importance. "This mystery is great," writes Paul: "but I speak in regard of Christ and of the church." The word "mystery" has here the usual New Testament meaning. It does not denote something mysterious and cryptic and difficult to understand, but something once hidden and now revealed. By a "mys-

tery" which is "great," Paul indicates a reality which is
well known and of profound significance. All Christians
should understand and remember that marriage is hal-
lowed by the fact that it is a symbol of the union of Christ
with his church, and should regulate their conduct in accordance with their knowledge of a truth so sublime.

"Nevertheless," Paul continues—that is, not to dwell
on this spiritual and supernal analogy, but to return to the
thought of the obvious and mutual obligations of husbands
and wives—"do ye also severally love each one his own
wife even as himself." No husband is exempt from the
rule. He is to love his wife as being a very part of himself. "And let the wife see that she fear her husband,"
that is, hold him in reverent, obedient, affectionate regard.
It is only by such mutual submission and loyalty that the
Christian home can be maintained, and the Christian
home is the most sacred, the most blessed institution upon
earth, the most gracious gift of God to man.

2. CHILDREN AND PARENTS   Ch. 6:1-4

1 Children, obey your parents in the Lord: for this is
right. 2 Honor thy father and mother (which is the first
commandment with promise), 3 that it may be well with
thee, and thou mayest live long on the earth. 4 And, ye
fathers, provoke not your children to wrath: but nurture
them in the chastening and admonition of the Lord.

The family is the unit in the social structure; it is the
strength and glory of the church. However, the peace
and the very existence of family life can be preserved only
as the members of each household respect their mutual
rights and perform their reciprocal obligations. Therefore, when Paul has set forth the duties of wives and husbands, he turns to enforce the right relations of children
and parents. The subjection and reverence of the wife
are to be in response to self-sacrificing love on the part of
the husband. So the loving obedience of the child is to

be encouraged by the sympathetic and considerate discipline of the parent.

"Children, obey your parents in the Lord." This duty of filial obedience has been recognized in all ages and lands and among all peoples. It is also true that the neglect of this duty has been lamented by writers of all nations and times. The present is therefore not unique as an age in which there is great need of emphasizing this command of the apostle.

There are, of course, many homes in which reverence and respect for parents produce an atmosphere of purity and unity in which young lives develop in safety and beauty.

Furthermore, it is evident that times and customs change and no children should be expected to follow minutely all the habits and ways of their parents. Again it must be admitted that parents may at times be unfair and unreasonable in their requirements and demands.

Nevertheless, when all this has been said, it is not difficult to show that in the present vaunted "revolt of youth," and in the acts and attitudes of many children, there is shown a restiveness under restraint, a reckless disregard of parental advice, and a lawless demand for freedom, which threaten family life and produce some of the most serious problems of the day.

Under such conditions this word of divine wisdom may well be repeated and enforced: "Children, obey your parents." The term "obey" describes a "readiness to hear"; the "listening ear of unhesitating attention"; not only obedience in action, but a willingness to heed counsel, to weigh words of advice, and then gladly to shape one's course under the accepted guidance of more mature minds.

Both parents are included in the command. Mothers as well as fathers are to be obeyed. Their wills are supposed to be in harmony, their directions to be in accord. Yet the obedience is to be not only in view of the relation of parents to one another, or even of children to their parents. The obedience is to be "in the Lord." It is to be in view of the fact that the children belong to Christ. They are members of his body. They recognize him as their Master. Their obedience is to be Christian obedience. It is to be rendered because of such spiritual sanctions, and as impelled by such high motives. Children are to act in accordance with the will of the Lord and in accordance with his divine ordinances.

"For this is right," the apostle insists. It is not only becoming and befitting. It is not only according to custom or a kindly concession to an ancient prejudice; it is "right." It accords with the law of God. It is one of the Ten Commandments, wisely given for the moral guidance of man and embodying principles of life which are divine in their sanctions and changeless in their validity.

"Honor thy father and mother." Obedience properly springs from reverence and respect. The command to obey issues from the command to "honor" and is enforced by it. It is thus to be the honor, not of weak emotion, but of practical loyalty.

This Fifth Commandment which Paul here quoted is declared to be "the first commandment with promise." The exact meaning of the statement it is impossible to determine. It might mean that it is a commandment of first importance, and one to which a promise is attached. It may indicate that while the Ten Commandments were followed by many other precepts in the law of Moses, this is the first to which a specific promise is attached.

While the precise idea is not evident, the main teaching and force of the words are perfectly plain: This divine command is coupled with a divine assurance of blessing to all by whom it is obeyed. The commandment is given, "that it may be well with thee, and thou mayest live long on the earth." This law, therefore, has promise for "the life which now is," as well as for "that which is to come." Obedience to parents assures prosperity and good health.

This is to be taken as literally true. There are exceptions to all such rules, but the promise is being verified by the history of countless families in all lands. Obedience of children to wise and loving Christian parents results in habits of industry, of self-control and self-respect, of faithfulness and kindness, which are absolute guarantees of success and of long continuance of life.

The original promise made to Israel, with a reference to the "land" of promise, was in accordance with a principle which not only applied to the family life of Hebrews and of early Christians, but which is true at the present time as well. Temporal blessings and length of days may be expected normally by children who render obedience and honor to their parents.

On the other hand, parents must show themselves worthy to be obeyed. "Children, obey your parents" was not designed as a weapon to be placed in the hands of godless tyrants. The duty of children toward parents is not more real than that of parents toward children. Submission on the one side is no more necessary than gentleness and sympathetic guidance on the other. Therefore Paul immediately adds, "And, ye fathers, provoke not your children to wrath: but nurture them in the chastening and admonition of the Lord." Fathers are here named, either as representing both parents or because to them in particular the discipline and government of the home belong. However, it is not intended that the rights and needed influence of mothers are to be overlooked.

The duty of fathers is expressed both negatively and positively. First, "provoke not your children to wrath." The word denotes not only the causing of irritation and exasperation by parental exactions and demands, but, further, the awakening of anger by treatment that is harsh and oppressive and unfair. This is not to say that a father must never refuse to allow a child to have its own way, or must permit a child to do wrong for fear of arousing its anger. Nothing could be more unkind than to let a child believe that by an exhibition of temper it can secure anything it may desire. This is the abdication of parental authority. This is to make a child the constant victim of self-indulgence and caprice.

What the exhortation does forbid is such unfair treatment, such cruel demands, such a selfish insistence upon authority, as to awaken in the heart of a child a rankling sense of injustice.

Discipline, however, must be exercised; therefore the positive side of parental duty toward children is this: "Nurture them in the chastening and admonition of the Lord." This watchful care, this constant training will be by way of "chastening" and "admonition." The former is not to be understood as merely denoting punishment, but rather as signifying education by means of discipline, and instruction by means of correction. "Admonition" denotes training by verbal reproof or remonstrance. It implies that there are faults in the nature of a child, and that a father is negligent of his obvious duty if he fails to remonstrate with a child for errors in the past or to counsel him as to temptations in the future.

However, all such restraint and warning must be "of the Lord." They must be in accordance with the will of the Lord. They must be by those who recognize their relation to the Lord. Indeed, they must be such as parents exercise in the very place of the Lord, as his representatives, as those who are administering his laws, as those who are the messengers of his grace.

Such Christian nurture is one of the supreme needs of the day. The great peril is that children may be allowed to grow up with no respect for authority, with no reverence for age, with no knowledge of Christian standards, with no habits of deference and self-control. To meet this need parents may gladly welcome the help of school and church. However, they should be impressed anew with the fact that the most important training ground for the education and discipline of children is the Christian home.

3. SERVANTS AND MASTERS   Ch. 6:5-9

5 Servants, be obedient unto them that according to the flesh are your masters, with fear and trembling, in singleness of your heart, as unto Christ; 6 not in the way of eyeservice, as menpleasers; but as servants of Christ, doing the will of God from the heart; 7 with good will doing service, as unto the Lord, and not unto men: 8 knowing that whatsoever good thing each one doeth, the same shall he receive again from the Lord, whether he be bond or free. 9 And, ye masters, do the same things unto them, and forbear threatening: knowing that he who is both their Master and yours is in heaven, and there is no respect of persons with him.

The third typical relation in the family is that of servants and masters. The first was that of wives and husbands; the second, of children and parents. In each case Paul taught that the particular relation involves mutual duties. Submission on the part of the wife is in view of self-sacrificing devotion on the part of the husband. Obedience is to be rendered by children, but parents must fulfill the obligation of loving Christian care. So here, servants must be obedient and loyal, but masters must be just, considerate, and kind.

In all three cases the duties which these mutual relationships involve are enforced by an appeal to the highest motives. Thus servants are to be faithful because in reality they are rendering service to Christ, and masters are to be just and sympathetic because they have in heaven a Master to whom they and their servants belong, and by whom both they and their servants are to be judged. That is to say, both servants and masters are to regulate their conduct by Christian standards and are to act in accordance with Christian principles.

It is to be remembered that the servants here concerned were "bondservants," slaves, and it is instructive to note how Christianity dealt with slavery, the most iniquitous institution of man. In the days of Paul it was universally accepted and approved by the most advanced civilization of the world. Furthermore, it was attended by abuses and abominations too revolting to detail. However, Christ and his followers attempted no political or social revolution; they led no armed revolt; they did not encourage disloyalty or lawlessness. What they did was to undermine the institution of slavery by advocating the principles of Christ. The gospel proved to be a proclamation of emancipation. Slavery must ultimately disappear when men accept the doctrines of human equality and spiritual brotherhood and the Lordship of Christ.

While Paul is here presenting the mutual duties of slaves and masters, the instructions he gives are of supreme importance to "servants" of all classes and conditions. These duties are not less but more obviously obligatory upon all employees and all employers in all lands and times. In this industrial age the injunctions of the apostle are more needed than ever before. The present relations between labor and capital, between masters and servants, are so vital and yet so strained that nothing but the adoption of the principles advocated by Paul can save the modern world from universal disaster.

First of all, then, the Christian profession requires on the part of servants and employees the recognition of constituted authority, and specifically the duty of obedience: "Servants, be obedient unto them that according to the flesh are your masters." These masters "according to the flesh," as distinct from a Master who is in heaven, may be taken to include all who in domestic and industrial and civil relationships have a legal right to direct, to command, and to control the activities of other men.

Obedience to such lawful masters must be rendered with an eager solicitude to accomplish any task assigned. It must be "with fear and trembling," that is, with respect for the rightful authority of the master and keen anxiety to leave no duty undone.

Furthermore, obedience is to be rendered "in singleness

of . . . heart," not in hypocrisy and pretense, but with a sincere and undivided purpose, "as unto Christ"—that is, as though it were being rendered unto the Lord himself.

This obedience, further, is to be "not in the way of eyeservice, as menpleasers." "Eyeservice" is a picturesque description of the conduct of servants who work well when being watched, but who are idle or careless when the master is absent. "Menpleasers" defines those who for selfish ends, even while unfaithful, seek to curry favor with their masters. They are mentioned in contrast with those who render obedience "as servants of Christ, doing the will of God from the heart; with good will doing service, as unto the Lord, and not unto men." Labor is immeasurably dignified by such considerations as these. The task of the humblest slave may be ennobled by being rendered in such a way as to please Christ, with such good will, with such hearty readiness and zeal, as to merit the approval of the Lord.

Such toil will receive his recognition and his reward. One can serve an earthly master with this absolute assurance, "knowing that whatsoever good thing each one doeth, the same shall he receive again from the Lord, whether he be bond or free." This sentence contains a forceful expression of the certainty and sufficiency of the reward. The "good thing" done is represented as itself given back to the doer. The meaning must be that the good thing is known to the Lord, is remembered by him, and from him will receive full acknowledgment and recompense.

The time of this just and final reward is usually described as being at the Lord's return. It is then that he will reckon with his servants. Then full justice will be done to each, "whether he be bond or free." All human distinctions will then be forgotten. The question then will not be as to what social position one held, but as to whether he was faithful in his task. Even a slave in the corrupt conditions of the first century could so live as to receive at last from his master the glad words of praise, "Well done, good and faithful servant: . . . enter thou into the joy of thy lord."

On the other hand, the obligation of right conduct and fair dealing rests upon the master quite as truly as upon the slave, and upon the employer as well as upon the employee. In fact the responsibility is even greater, for the master is usually in the position of superior privilege and power and advantage, and "to whomsoever much is given, of him shall much be required." If it is the duty of "servants" to be faithful and loyal, so it is the duty of masters to be kindly and considerate, seeking the highest welfare of those by whom they are served.

This duty is presented positively and negatively. First, masters are told what to do: "And, ye masters, do the same things unto them." They are to act on the same Christian principles; they are to show the same consideration and good will. They are to consult the welfare of their servants as they expect their servants to regard their own. They are to apply to the treatment even of slaves the Golden Rule of their Master, "Whatsoever ye would that men should do unto you, even so do ye also unto them."

Then they are told what not to do: "Forbear threatening." This command was greatly needed. Slaves were regarded as little better than beasts. It was thought necessary to keep them in their place and to rule them by the fear of punishment, by threats of torture and death. Even at the present time it is possible for employers to keep employees in fear—by threats of lower wages or loss of employment, by the dread of hunger and of want. "Threatening" implies coercion and compulsion by those in a position to exercise tyranny. It should be entirely displaced by sympathy for the servant and by reverence for the divine Master to whom both servants and masters must render account "knowing," as Paul writes, "that he who is both their Master and yours is in heaven." This exalted Christ is in the place of supreme power. He knows and he will recompense. He will punish and he will reward. His judgment is with absolute justice. "There is no respect of persons with him." He shows no partiality and no favoritism. He is not influenced by regard for social place or human power. He condemns unkindness in a master quite as severely as unfaithfulness in a servant. Therefore a Christian master will show toward his servants that unfailing justice and mercy which he expects to receive from his Master and his Lord. Such mutual regard and loyalty on the part of servants and masters cannot fail to secure domestic tranquillity and industrial prosperity and peace.

D. THE CHRISTIAN WARFARE
Ch. 6:10-20

10 Finally, be strong in the Lord, and in the strength of his might. 11 Put on the whole armor of God, that ye may be able to stand against the wiles of the devil. 12 For our wrestling is not against flesh and blood, but against the principalities, against the powers, against the world-rulers of this darkness, against the spiritual hosts *of wickedness in the heavenly* places. *13 Wherefore take up the whole armor of God, that ye may be able to withstand in the evil day, and, having done all, to stand. 14 Stand therefore, having girded your loins with truth, and having put on the breastplate of righteousness, 15 and having shod your feet with the preparation of the gospel of peace; 16 withal taking up the shield of faith, wherewith ye shall be able to quench all the fiery darts of the evil* one. *17 And take the helmet of salvation, and the sword of the Spirit, which is the word of God: 18 with all prayer and supplication praying at all seasons in the Spirit, and watching thereunto in all perseverance and supplication for all the saints, 19 and on my behalf, that utterance may be given unto me in opening my mouth, to make known with boldness the mystery of the gospel, 20 for which I am an ambassador in chains; that in it I may speak boldly, as I ought to speak.*

The Christian life is a continual conflict. Battle must be waged daily against the most relentless foes. In this warfare there is no discharge. The demand is for courage, for determination, for ceaseless vigilance, for undaunted hope. All this is but a commonplace of spiritual experience.

Yet there are those by whom the truth is forgotten. There are even those by whom it is denied. They are ready to maintain that what they term victory is merely a passive acceptance of a divine process. To the mind of Paul the need for struggle was ever present, and he never ceases to warn his readers of their peril, their duty, and their call to win for Christ the victory and to win from him the crown.

If in any of his writings reference to spiritual warfare might be omitted, it would most naturally be in the epistle to the Ephesians. The first half of the letter displays the predestinating grace of God, giving life to those who are spiritually dead, and raising them up with Christ, and enabling them to sit "in the heavenly places, in Christ Jesus." The last half of the epistle contains exhortations to manifest the most elementary virtues in the common relations of life. However, Paul closes this letter with the most striking, the most detailed, the most instructive reference to Christian warfare which the Bible anywhere contains. It is the climax of the epistle as well as its close.

Paul insists that a position "in the heavenlies" cannot be retained without conflict, and that in all spheres of experience Christians are called upon to wage unceasing war. The last of these spheres to be mentioned has been that of the home. There is something almost startling in the sudden passing from the peaceful scene of the Christian home to the field of battle with its clash of arms and its overhanging clouds.

There are three special features in this notable paragraph: the character of the foe, the description of the armor, and the summons to prayerful sympathy with fellow soldiers in the strife.

It is in view of the appalling character of the enemy that the call to arms is sounded. "Finally," or "henceforth," writes the apostle as he begins the last of his stirring appeals, "be strong in the Lord, and in the strength of his might." Christ is the one inexhaustible Source from which strength can be drawn by obedient trust. One can "be strong," only "in the Lord," but the energetic "strength of his might" is sure to be put forth in behalf of those who by faith are united with him.

"Put on the whole armor of God," that is, the armor which God supplies. The picture of the Christian as a soldier armed for conflict is familiar to every reader of the New Testament. The emphasis here is upon the necessary completeness of his equipment. It is not only the armor, but "the whole armor" that must be taken. That is to say, victory depends not only on the strength which the Lord gives, but upon the faithfulness of the Christian in accepting every instrument and implement which God offers to aid in this mortal combat.

Such strength and such weapons are needed because the enemy is pictured as none other than the devil, the great adversary, the slanderous accuser, the malignant foe of the followers of Christ. He is pictured here as waging his warfare with deception and strategems and crafty assaults. The whole armor is needed that the Christian "may be able to stand against the wiles of the devil."

So this conflict is described as one in which no merely human opponents are to be met; nor is it against the devil alone: "For our wrestling [our personal, individual, hand-to-hand encounter] is not against flesh and blood, but against the principalities, against the powers, against the world-rulers of this darkness, against the spiritual hosts of wickedness in the heavenly places." The New Testament indicates the personality of Satan, but this does not imply omnipotence or omniscience or omnipresence. These are attributes of God, not of his adversary. However, the devil is here pictured as in command of spirit forces which

are characterized by evil and which rule in the sphere of
the world's moral darkness. These forces are endeavoring
to dislodge the Christian from his high position in the
heavenly places to which he has been raised in union with
Christ.

All that these words may mean it is difficult if not dangerous to conjecture. How far figures of speech are to be
pressed, what is the real nature of the spirit world, none
can confidently state. Suffice it to believe that no matter
how high and heavenly may be the spiritual experiences
they enjoy, Christians are never beyond the assaults of the
most seductive and satanic influences. They are ever
liable to attack by enemies of the soul with which, in their
own strength, they are utterly unable to cope. Lusts and
weaknesses and passions, which are familiar and common, are sufficiently deadly in themselves to fill the soul
with terror, even aside from all speculations upon the
sphere of the superhuman and the unseen.

It is because of such foes that the apostle urges the
Christian to "take up the whole armor of God." It is in
order—and it is the only way—to be able "to withstand
in the evil day," in the hour of temptation, in the moment
of moral peril, and to withstand all the opposing forces,
"and, having done all," having overcome the foe and
driven him from the field, "to stand" victorious, un-
wounded, unmoved, and unafraid.

This armor, piece by piece, the writer now proceeds to
designate. "Stand therefore, having girded your loins
with truth." The girdle or military belt was no mere orna-
ment, but a necessary part of the equipment. As such it
is mentioned first. It was used to hold other pieces of
armor in place, and to secure for the soldier a proper
carriage and at the same time freedom of action. The
virtue which the girdle was taken to represent is "truth,"
that is, truthfulness, sincerity—downright frankness and
honesty with ourselves, with one another, and with God.
It is particularly in this last relation that "truth" is abso-

lutely vital. In our dealing with God, there must be no disguise and no deceit if we are to win in the spiritual conflict in which all are engaged. Any conscious insincerity or attempt to excuse a known fault produces moral weakness which invites defeat. On the other hand, nothing inspires more courage than the consciousness of being in right relation to God.

"The breastplate of righteousness" naturally is next to be named. It is closely related to the girdle of truth, for righteousness here denotes uprightness, or moral integrity. As the breastplate, or cuirass, protected the heart and other vital organs, so one who binds himself about with a determined loyalty to the holy will and law of God is secure against the deadly thrusts of the tempter. A man who is conscious of being in the wrong is usually a coward; a man who knows that he is right can withstand a multitude and enters the conflict without fear.

The strong military sandals not only protected the feet of the warrior but enabled him to stand in slippery places and to move with quick and certain step. So the Christian soldier needs to be equipped for battle with that "preparation" which only "the gospel," with its message of peace, can give. It is peace with God through our Lord Jesus Christ which enables us to stand firmly in difficult places, and to move swiftly in opposing the enemies of the soul.

Furthermore, as his main defense, the Roman legionary carried a huge doorlike "shield," usually made of wood and covered with leather, fully four feet in height, and capable of giving protection against weapons of practically every kind. For the Christian warrior "faith" forms such a shield. Therefore the exhortation continues, "Withal," or "in addition to all this," "taking up the shield of faith, wherewith ye shall be able to quench all the fiery darts of the evil one."

The reference is to arrows tipped with tow, dipped in pitch, and set on fire before they were discharged. These "fiery darts," striking the shield, would fall extinguished and harmless at the warrior's feet. Thus firm and unwavering confidence in God, a continual reliance upon him, affords for the believer a safe protection against those swift arrows of temptation which might inflame the heart with anger or with lust.

"And take the helmet of salvation," the martial order adds. The word for "take" differs from that used in reference to the shield. It means to "accept," and thus to receive from God's hand something he has prepared for us. "Salvation" is such a gift. It is to be accepted as a present possession. Hereafter we shall receive it in its perfection. However, the assurance that it is already ours—that we are now saved and are being kept by the power of God—this will be our sure protection, like the gleaming, crested helmet which covered the head of the triumphant warrior.

All this spiritual armor mentioned by the apostle was for purposes of defense. The one weapon of offense he now names. It will suffice. There is need of no other. It is "the sword of the Spirit, which is the word of God." The gospel message placed in the hands of the Christian warrior must be firmly grasped and used with skill. All the truth revealed in Christ will be of priceless value in the spiritual conflict. With this weapon, and with this weapon alone, the true knight of the cross can ward off every attack of the adversary, and even put to flight opposing hosts of evil.

Such is the armor graciously given by the King to make victory possible and to enable each of his servants to win the crown of life. The apostle now closes his portrayal of the Christian warfare with a description of the spirit in which the conflict is to be waged. It is the spirit of sympathetic, watchful intercession. By this instrument the warrior keeps in constant blessed communication with his divine Commander.

In addition to the armor God provides, or in the use of this divine panoply, one who is to stand fast must have recourse to earnest constant prayer: "With all prayer and supplication," with every form of worshipful approach to God and with every variety of request from him. "Praying at all seasons" means at every time of crisis, in every hour of need. "Praying . . . in the Spirit" defines the character of true prayer; it is offered under the guidance of the Spirit, in fellowship with the Spirit, in dependence upon the Spirit. It is this which gives reality and power to Christian intercession and supplication. There must be also vigilance and persistence in prayer. One must be "watching thereunto in all perseverance." The spirit must be that of sleeplessness and also of importunity, of one who will "pray, and not . . . faint."

Nor must this prayer be for himself alone. One fights more valiantly and more gallantly when he remembers that he is not alone. Near him is the unseen Commander, to whom he lifts his cry for strength, but around him are countless warriors, some hard pressed and sorely bestead, some ready to give him encouragement and help, but all in need of his sympathetic prayers. Therefore the Christian warrior is urged to make "supplication for all the saints," that is, for all believers, for all the people of God, for all the army of the redeemed.

Specifically, however, prayer is asked by the writer for himself. "Pray on my behalf," he shouts to his embattled friends. He has been taken captive by men, but he is "a prisoner [for the sake] of Christ." He is not discouraged. He can fight in his very dungeon. In his imprisonment he can bear a message as an ambassador, representing his Royal Captain. "Pray," he is saying, "on my behalf, that utterance may be given unto me in opening my mouth, to make known . . . the mystery of the gospel." By "the mystery of the gospel" he means the glorious revelation that it contains, its worldwide mission, its eternal issues, its life-giving power. "For which [gospel]," writes the apostle, "I am an ambassador in chains." Strange decoration this, for a legate of the King, yet pray on for me that on this theme, in the sphere of this glorious gospel message, "I may speak boldly, as I ought to speak."

Thus Paul requests prayer for himself, but only that he may be able to bear witness to the grace and goodness of his Lord. The aged warrior is undaunted. He has "fought the good fight," he has "kept the faith." Yet he finds in his Roman prison an arena in which he can win further laurels for his Lord, a battlefield on which he can gain new victories, a royal court where he can deliver a deathless message from his Master. He is not self-confident. He has no strength of his own. He needs help from heaven. Therefore he signals to his fellow soldiers in far-off Asia. He asks them to unite with him in earnest request that the Captain of their salvation will grant him strength and grace, that in his present post of duty he may lift to his lips with new courage the gospel trumpet, to sound forth boldly the glad tidings of salvation and abiding victory in the name of Jesus Christ his Lord.

IV
THE CONCLUSION
Ch. 6:21-24

21 But that ye also may know my affairs, how I do, Tychicus, the beloved brother and faithful minister in the Lord, shall make known to you all things: 22 whom I have sent unto you for this very purpose, that ye may know our state, and that he may comfort your hearts.

23 Peace be to the brethren, and love with faith, from God the Father and the Lord Jesus Christ. 24 Grace be with all them that love our Lord Jesus Christ with a love incorruptible.

The matchless message is now complete. Paul is about to send it across the seas to his Christian friends in the distant province of Asia. How much farther it was to go no one could have dreamed. On across the centuries it has been carried, on to all the lands and nations of the earth, giving gladness and guidance to the people of God; opening up vistas of divine truth; revealing the grace of the Father, the love of the Son, the power of the Holy Spirit; revealing the dignity and destiny of the church, the bride of Christ, redeemed by his blood, commissioned to proclaim his gospel, and looking in eagerness and love for his return.

Paul adds to his message only a word to commend the messenger by whom it was being sent, and to pronounce a benediction upon those by whom it would be read.

This messenger was Tychicus. He seems to have been a native of Asia. He joined Paul on his third missionary journey, was with the apostle in his present imprisonment at Rome, was his companion during his closing years, and

seems to have been sent by the apostle to Ephesus to relieve Timothy when the latter was summoned to Rome to
receive his great master's last farewell.

He is here described as "the beloved brother," that is a
loved member of the Christian brotherhood, and as a
"faithful minister," that is, more particularly a "minister"
to Paul. The latter word is easily misunderstood. It does
not here designate a church officer but one who was a
servant in any capacity. Every church officer of whatever
rank should be the servant of his fellow Christians, even
as the humblest Christian may minister to the saints.

Tychicus had the high honor of rendering personal help
to Paul, as his companion in travel, as his helper in the
days of his imprisonment, and now as his messenger to the
churches of Asia.

The purpose of his mission was to bear this priceless
epistle. However, he was further to cheer the readers
with personal and intimate messages concerning the situation and plans of the apostle. "That ye also may know
my affairs, how I do, Tychicus, the beloved brother and
faithful minister in the Lord, shall make known to you all
things." Evidently, from references in other epistles written near this time, Paul had high hopes of being released
from his imprisonment in Rome and of visiting his dear
friends in the Asiatic churches. It was probably with this
prospect in view that Paul writes in this passage, "Whom
I have sent unto you for this very purpose, that ye may
know our state, and that he may comfort your hearts."
Such comfort Tychicus undoubtedly was able to convey.
However, in his lowly service as the bearer of a brief letter
to Asia from a prisoner of Rome he was rendering a priceless service to the world and winning for himself an immortality of fame.

The closing benediction of Paul reechoes the great
words which resound with heavenly music through all the
passages he has composed. "Peace," "love," "grace"—
these notes are combined in endless variety and in moving

melodies. They further are given an impressive majesty by being linked as here with the names of "God the Father" and "the Lord Jesus Christ."

Here peace is invoked on the Christian brotherhood—peace with God, peace with men, the peace of God, peace in the heart, the peace that "passeth all understanding." "Peace be to the brethren," writes the apostle, "and love with faith." The love for which he prays is love for the brethren, that love which accompanies faith, even Christian love, which reveals itself where faith is, and by which faith works. These blessings are traced to their twofold source in "God the Father and the Lord Jesus Christ."

The last note of the benediction was the first word of the opening salutation, and has been the keynote of the whole epistle: "Grace be with all them that love our Lord Jesus Christ." "Grace," the unmerited favor of God—grace which Paul traces back to a purpose formed in eternity, which he finds manifested in the redeeming work of Christ, which through the church will be manifested in the ages to come; grace to Gentiles and Jews; grace in its boundless fullness—that this may be known by all them that love Christ is Paul's final prayer. Yet he can ask this only for those in whom love for Christ is true and abiding—for "them that love our Lord Jesus Christ with a love incorruptible" are his words. May such love as "knows neither change, diminution, nor decay" be granted to all who read this epistle, that they may experience increasingly the riches of grace in Christ Jesus.